"My Toughest Mentor"

"My Toughest Mentor"

Theodore Roethke
and William Carlos Williams
(1940–1948)

Robert Kusch

Lewisburg
Bucknell University Press
London: Associated University Presses

Associated University Presses
440 Forsgate Drive
Cranbury, NJ 08512

Associated University Presses
16 Barter Street
London WC1A 2AH, England

Associated University Presses
P.O. Box 338, Port Credit
Mississauga, Ontario
Canada L5G 4L8

PS
3535
.O39
Z655
1999

The paper used in this publication meets the requirements of the American National Standard for Permanence of Paper for Printed Library Materials Z39.48-1984.

Library of Congress Cataloging-in-Publication Data

Kusch, Robert, 1934–
    My toughest mentor : Theodore Roethke and William Carlos Williams (1940–1948) / Robert Kusch.
        p.   cm.
    Includes bibliographical references and index.
    ISBN 0-8387-5406-6 (alk. paper)
    1. Roethke, Theodore, 1908–1963—Criticism and interpretation.
    2. Williams, William Carlos, 1883–1963—Friends and associates.
    3. Roethke, Theodore, 1908–1963—Friends and associates.
    4. Williams, William Carlos, 1883–1963—Correspondence.
    5. Williams, William Carlos, 1883–1963—Influence. 6. Roethke, Theodore, 1908–1963—Correspondence. 7. Poets, American—20th century—Correspondence. 8. Poetics. I. Title.
    PS3535.O39Z655   1999
    811'.5209—dc21   98-50628
                                                                          CIP

To Marcella

Contents

Acknowledgements

Earlier versions of chapters one and two have appeared in the *Journal of Modern Literature* 12:2 (1985) and 16:1 (1989), respectively. They are used with permission of Indiana University Press.

Grateful acknowledgement is made for permission to quote from the following works:

The Autobiography of William Carlos Williams. Copyright 1948 and 1951 by William Carlos Williams. Reprinted by permission of New Directions Publishing Corporation and Carcanet Press Ltd.

Collected Poems: Volume II, 1939–1962. Copyright 1944, 1953, Copyright © 1962 by William Carlos Williams. Copyright © 1988 by William Eric Williams and Paul H. Williams. Reprinted by permission of New Directions Publishing Corporation and Carcanet Press Ltd.

I Wanted to Write a Poem. Copyright © 1958 by William Carlos Williams. Reprinted by permission of New Directions Publishing Corporation and Carcanet Press Ltd.

Paterson. Copyright © 1946, 1948, 1949 by William Carlos Williams. Reprinted by permission of New Directions Publishing Corporation and Carcanet Press Ltd.

Selected Essays. Copyright © 1954 by William Carlos Williams. Reprinted by permission of New Directions Publishing Corporation and Carcanet Press Ltd.

Previously unpublished material by William Carlos Williams. Copyright © by Paul H. Williams and the Estate of William Carlos Williams. Used by permission of New Directions Publishing Corporation, agents.

"Ballad of the Clairvoyant Widow," copyright 1941 by Theodore Roethke; "Cuttings," copyright 1948 by Theodore Roethke; "Cuttings (later)" copyright 1948 by Theodore Roethke; "Judge Not," copyright 1947 by The University of the South; "The Minimal,"

* * *

In collecting materials for this book, I have received generous assistance from the staffs of Beinecke Rare Book and Manuscript Library, Yale University, and Suzzallo Library, University of Washington, especially Janet Ness and Karyl Winn. Arlene Bubrow and Linda Kozusko in the Department of English at Rutgers University rendered all kinds of substantial help in bringing the text to completion. John Wheatcroft read the manuscript and sharpened its focus with his excellent critical suggestions. My wife, Marcella, gave me space and light, and made these into a sustaining trust that is more than I can repay.

Introduction

F<small>EW POETS ACHIEVE THE CONTINUITY AND DIRECTION OF THEIR MA-</small>jor poems without some inner conflict, and many exorcise their uncertainty by developing a "reader" whose sense of the future they can trust. In modern poetry, the best-known example is T. S. Eliot's showing a draft of *The Waste Land* to Ezra Pound, but we know that Yeats, Joyce, H. D., and William Carlos Williams also brought their work to Pound, who spoke for the next generation of critics in his notations. Williams once compared his first meeting with Pound to the difference between "B. C. and A. D.,"[1] and he engaged in one of Pound's many vocations by becoming a prolific commentator on the work of young poets, several of whom were just discovering a language they could claim as their own. Allen Ginsberg and Denise Levertov have spoken at length of Williams's involvement with decisive changes in their work, but Williams offers a longer, more complicated, and interesting history than even their stories can measure. In the fall of 1957, when Robert Lowell was bringing such poems as "Skunk Hour" and "Memories of West Street and Lepke" closer to the immediacy of conversation, he wrote Williams a series of warm, personal letters, saying at the close of one: "I feel more and more technically indebted to you, growing young in my forties."[2] And Theodore Roethke, exploring the instinctive sources of his language during the years of World War II, has left an important record of Williams's discernment and support.

"You're my toughest mentor," Roethke wrote in a letter to Williams on November 11, 1942, two years after their first meeting.[3] Although he meant it as a compliment, Roethke was clearly summarizing his relationship with Williams and involving himself further in the long process of self-criticism and growth. During those years, Roethke had managed to convert almost everyone to a view of his future by the promise of his first book, *Open House.* Williams, too, could imagine a future for Roethke's talent, but not for the studied measures and oblique confrontations of these first poems. Roethke, for reasons I will discuss later, was not discouraged. He kept on sending Williams food—smoked fish and cheeses, mostly—and more poems. The poems themselves never attempt to assume Williams's voice, but they do move toward Williams's emphasis on the language of common speech, and they begin to explore, as Williams would recommend, those histories embedded in "the less known side" of the self.[4] Roethke dedicated his third book, *Praise to the End*, to Kenneth Burke and Williams, and while Burke's role in Roethke's development has been generally emphasized, Williams's contribution remains less clear. Yet Roethke was acknowledging a debt, not obscure to him, in placing Williams alongside Burke, and it is this debt I want to explore.[5] Williams knew Roethke for several years before Roethke met Burke, and his view of the unrealized opportunities in Roethke's art, evident from the beginning of their correspondence, suggests that he often read Roethke's future better than Roethke read it himself. As Roethke began to discover his past in the image of what he might become, he also understood that Williams's dissatisfactions could not finally be separated from his loyalty. Their letters witness the energy they brought to their art; they also record Roethke's growth and Williams's attempt to define what he felt to be Roethke's authentic voice. As they stand now, many still unpublished, the letters appear like islands in an archipelago: they rest on a much larger base than is immediately visible and they are defined by the space that separates them. To measure some part of their depth and cross that space is the object of this study.

"My Toughest Mentor"

1

"The less known side"

In the late thirties, Williams was just beginning his career as a reader before university audiences, and one of his first invitations came from Roethke, who was teaching at Pennsylvania State College. The date was set for Sunday, May 12, 1940. At the age of fifty-five, Williams had just published his *Complete Collected Poems* (1938) and, though he could not know it then, had just finished one of the most prolific decades of his life. From 1930 to 1940, Williams brought out nine books and, on the eve of World War II, was well into shaping *Paterson*. Although he would begin a long letter to Norman Holmes Pearson in the fall of 1938 by complaining that he had not written anything for over a year and that he was beset by the desperation of middle age, he would add, as the letter turned over, that he felt a surprising power in the language of his complaint: "I want to be drunk and I am beginning to feel drunk. With the only drink I know that intoxicates me: words at flow."[1] But he also wanted the immediate presence of an audience. Readings gave him the opportunity to test the energy of his poems and, unexpectedly at times, his own durability. So Williams in the *Autobiography:*

> At Penn State College one year, bidden by Ted Roethke and Bob Wetterau, Ted gave Floss and me a steak and trimmings with an excellent Chambertin that nearly ruined me. I remember that talk (it was one of my first): for the first fifteen minutes of it I heard myself discoursing pleasantly, but what I was talking about was not at all what I had intended to say. At that moment my wits returned. It was a valuable experience. I found that from then on I should never be at a loss for words.[2]

Williams does not say it, but that this recovery should have happened before an academic audience is of some importance.

15

From his point of view, the academy had committed itself to the stature of T. S. Eliot, and not to have lost his words in this place became a victory over a much taller invisible enemy. Since Roethke had invited *him*, there was reason to hope that the cause of an American measure might at last receive a voice. And the significance of the invitation was not lost on the later Williams: most of the readings Williams records in the *Autobiography* are the ones before university audiences.

If Williams remembered the wine and his own recovery, Roethke remembered a very different episode. "We had a powerful lack of interest in each other's poetry," he would say to Allan Seager, commenting on the same evening.[3] For Williams, the reasons were not far to seek. At thirty-one, Roethke had not yet published his first book, though most of the poems that would appear in *Open House* (1941) had been completed and several had already appeared in the *Atlantic Monthly, Poetry, New Yorker,* and *Nation.* The style of these poems could hardly have won Williams's respect. With their rhymes, off-rhymes, and formal measures, Roethke's early poems resolve their conflicts in the orders of form and sound. Overall, the line determines the syntax and the stanza the thought: readers often feel they have entered a house furnished by many previous owners. On the Sunday he read at Penn State, Williams gave Roethke a one-page summary of his art, presumably to be used as background for the discussion that followed the reading. If Roethke did not know it already, Williams's statements would have told him a good deal about their differences:

> His [Williams's] rules for writing are very simple: to make something for relief comparable to the life he knows, i.e. not to offer terza rima to an Athenian.
>
> For this, first, to listen to the language that it may reveal itself: no line less native to the ear than he's heard spoken.
>
> Then, to raise without distortion to intensity by all means at his disposal: by metaphor which multiplies the echoes or by other formal emphasis.
>
> But never to twist a clause to fit a rhyme or pad a line for any reason but to seek to discover in the language what new pattern may be available to take it as it lies.

Finally to realize that the language is his own, a fertile branch of Elizabethan, new and almost unexplored in its resources for formal development today.

Whence, by his inventions, to make new raids on the inarticulate.[4]

Most of what is distinctive in Williams's work is reflected in these statements, and his use of the third person suggests the distance of one who has come from a far country—as, indeed, he thought he had. Seventeen years later in a letter to Roethke, Williams would recall that he thought himself "little more than a farm boy with no formal education" when he read that Sunday at Penn State, but the brevity and assurance of these statements offer evidence of a settled and confident practice.[5]

There had been some talk that evening of the creative potential of form, the two taking predictably opposite sides. Williams probably said that conventional forms could not express contemporary American experience, and Roethke, seeing in this a challenge to his art, replied that he had written a ballad that did—and he threatened to send it to Williams. The poem was, in fact, "The Ballad of the Clairvoyant Widow," and Roethke did send it a month or so later with a brief note explaining that "it was set up by a journeyman printer behind a saloon in Saginaw, Michigan. Neither of us was very good at proof reading at the time."[6] Following are the first eight stanzas:

Ballad of the Clairvoyant Widow

A kindly Widow Lady, who lived upon a hill,
Climbed to her attic window and gazed across the sill.

"Oh tell me, Widow Lady, what is it that you see,
As you look across my city, in God's country?"

"I see ten million windows, I see ten thousand streets
I see the traffic doing miraculous feats.

The lawyers all are cunning, the business men are fat,
Their wives go out on Sunday beneath the latest hat.

The kids play cops and robbers, the kids play mumbley-peg,
Some learn the art of thieving, and some grow up to beg:

The rich can play at polo, the poor can do the shag,
Professors are condoning the cultural lag.

I see a banker's mansion with twenty wood-grate fires,
Alone, his wife is grieving for what her heart desires.

Next door there is a love-nest of plaster board and tin,
The rats soon will be leaving, the snow will come in."[7]

On some level, the poem might have attracted Williams's attention even if he had not known Roethke. Jerome Mazzaro has said that many of Williams's poems are based on the mythic pattern of a descent into hell where the speaker meets a "wise old man" who offers him direction or "meaning." The wise old man may live in one of many guises—as teacher, philosopher, guide, or even "lucky idea"—and Williams himself was probably unaware of the archetypal relationship between the forms.[8] Nevertheless, Williams understood that Roethke's voice in the "Ballad" had taken a recognizable shape and that Roethke was sending the poem to suggest kinship as well as difference. Although the "Ballad" hardly offers a descent into hell, the conditions the widow "sees" in the first half of the poem are so chaotic that Williams could read some part of his own journey into Roethke's lines. In his reply, Williams begins by calling the poem "good"—later modified to "pretty good." As the letter gathers strength, he presents himself as friend, mentor, critic, and, not incidentally, wise old man:

June 30, 1940

Dear Roethke:

I like people who carry out their threats, you said you'd send me a poem written in the ballad form and you did send it and here it is and I have read it and it's good.
HOWEVER,
To me the effect is made diminutive by the form. The form represents a stable social order to me to the effect that though the poem implies a needed revolution of some sort to blast the hell out of something the FORM cries down what the poem wants to say. The form says, Well, anyhow bad as the world may be it's not bad as material for a poem—and a pretty good poem at that.
Now read what Clytemnestra says after she opens the curtains and

shows the crowd what she has done to her husband. That ain't diminutive.

Maybe I'm crying after the moon. Maybe I don't even know my own business. Maybe I'm trying to go beyond the limits of poetry for effects that belong in another field.

BUT

I don't think so. Go on writing good poems and prove to me that I'm cockeyed. I heard your poem read at the anti-fascist show in N.Y. ten or twelve days ago. It was well received and carried a dirty punch. Perhaps the suave blade cuts best because most subtly.

Thank you for sending the poem and thanks for ruining me that night with your excellent meats and drinks. I thought I should never be able to leave State College next day but I made it.

Sincerely yours

W. C. Williams[9]

Williams's point about Clytemnestra is particularly telling. She, too, is a widow, but what "ain't diminutive" is her will not just to "see" the consequences, but to re-create herself in the world of Agammemnon's death. No one could imagine her "living on a hill"; she has drawn the destructive act so far into herself that it has transformed her. Williams is not, in my view, just lecturing Roethke on the diminutions of form: Roethke's use of form suggests a larger hesitancy, a barrier distancing the speaker from that part of the self where destruction has its own compelling voice. With this distance, the language falters and the speaker exists in a dwindling circle of light. Roethke's widow is too kind.

What Roethke immediately made of this letter we do not know. Certainly, *Open House*, published in March 1941, does not reflect Williams's understanding of Clytemnestra. With all of their differing imperatives, however, both poets had passed a message— they were bound by a loyalty to each other's future. That loyalty soon surfaced when Roethke, reading a review of twelve poets by R. P. Blackmur in the Summer 1941 *Southern Review*, noticed that he and Williams had gone unmentioned. In the months following the appearance of *Open House*, reviewers such as Louise Bogan, Rolfe Humphries, W. H. Auden, and Yvor Winters had commented on Roethke's exceptional promise, and Roethke could hope that Blackmur would add his piece to the design. In preparing his review, Blackmur had begun with thirty-six books of poetry—*Open House* was undoubtedly among them—and had gradually reduced the number to twelve, a "precipitation," as he said, "formed spontaneously over a period of months."[10] The precipitation had also been by Eliot's publication of "The Dry Salvages" in the *Partisan Review* (May–June), an event Blackmur thought important to mention, even though Eliot was not under review. Blackmur's praise was by no means unrestrained, but he did offer the poem as the standard of excellence in contemporary poetry and discussed it prominently in his review. Alarmed by his exclusion and by the standard used to measure him, Roethke immediately thought of Williams, who had been excluded by a similar standard for most of his career. His note to Williams attempts to dismiss the event, while recording its considerable effect, with a rhyme:

> Old Dick the Prick Blackmur gave us both the go-by in the summer *Southern Review*: "Twelve Poets"—Aiken, Bishop, Cummings, Baker, Gregory, A. Y. Fisher & 5 young dribblenoses from New Directions. T.R.[11]

Williams clearly read the disappointment behind Roethke's attempt at humor, but he was by no means committed to Roethke's image, which unwittingly gave the critic too much power. He also resisted the pressure of Roethke's note to become one of "us." Williams could see himself as undiscovered, and perhaps still young, but he had grasped his place, inhabited it, and long before the beginning of *Paterson*, he had turned its history into the substance of his faith. In fact, more had happened: Paterson had given him the mountain, the landscape, river, and falls; he would return them as the giant, the women, courtship, and history. He saw that the event of the poem depended on something elusive and untamable, something Williams would call "the less known side" of the self, the source of Clytemnestra's rage and the language of the falls. His letter to Roethke on September 26, 1941, gives us a glimpse of Williams at the beginning of *Paterson*, and it also arrives at a critical turn in Roethke's career. With no plan for another book immediately before him, Roethke was ready to listen; he was also ready to allow his poems a wider range:

September 26, 1941

Dear Ted:

Weep not, Signor, over the lapses and tortuosities of Blackmur's disappointed mind. He is some sort of prince of the book, a latter day collegian. Forget him. That he has plums to distribute is merely a prerogative of his cast and means nothing more.

. . . .

I like the little "dribblenoses" whom New Directions prints. At least one of them is extremely flattering to my past. I tell you that you've got to write more and more fully out of the less known side of your nature if you are to be noticed. You are so damned much better than your position that I believe in you, that there is that to say out of your belly that can astonish—and you'll just have to astonish. Here I try to corrupt you. I haven't written a thing for the public eye, not a black(mur) eye to show in more than a year. Neither have you, that I have seen. You've got to dump it off the tail of a cart to make the waters rise . . .

Sincerely,
Bill[12]

The letter disposes of Blackmur by granting him a foreign title and a well-mapped country, but that gesture does not free Roethke from Williams's own scrutiny. Below the surface concern for getting noticed, Williams's real subject is growth, and the phrase "the less known side of your nature" offers a critique of *Open House* as well as a glimpse of Roethke's real frontier. The meanings inherent in that phrase were very much on Williams's mind in 1941–42 and were clarified in an article called "Advice to the Young Poet" where Williams configured an image and even a ritual for releasing "the less known side." The "Young Poet" is not named, but given the substance of Williams's advice to Roethke, it would be difficult to exclude Roethke from Williams's list of intended readers. "The less known side" now becomes a "dragon," which, like Lawrence's apocalyptic dragon, represents all that is vital, sensuous, and opposed to the forms knowledge has taken; as in Lawrence, the dragon is not to be supplanted or controlled, but given full voice and expression:

> All our efforts as writers and as men must be to release the enchained dragon within us. That it may not exist is no concern to the critic, we presume that it does. Unchained by whom? By ourselves, naturally, who else?
>
> There in all the colors of shells and crystals, as certain as chemistry, lives the thing we are, its connections with our senses afferent and direct. Subconsciously we cannot lie. But to give it efferent channels is another matter. It is an unwilling witness and there is no easy way to bring it to time—it is convenient to be a liar and too often the mark of culture—no way for the poet to unleash it but one open to all the destroying winds of the world and the world beyond the world.
>
> By words only can it be called up. Give your dragon the words and it will bear witness.
>
> Since when in modern times must we condone the effrontery of him who would predetermine the mould and complexion of the supernatural, delimiting that only as good which to him seems desirable?
>
> Your business is to see that all avenues of egress are kept open between what is inside you and the page. To do otherwise inaugurates a steady process of deterioration in a writer. And that isn't the half of it—unsuitable for this letter.[13]

The self Williams describes here is the same self that converts a routine doctor's visit into a ferociously aggressive act in "The Use of Force" and transforms a simple, almost sentimental ritual into a Dionysian orgy in "Burning the Christmas Greens." In both works, the social and professional conventions have been upheld, but the form of the work has been filled by a presence no one of the doctor's patients—or neighbors—would recognize. He never surprises himself, however; indeed, the surprise at the end of "The Use of Force" is the complete acceptance of the self in all of its consuming muscular rage. The "use" of force is finally to drive the self beyond the quotidian, to discover and record the shape of "the less known side."

Roethke probably did not see Williams's "Advice," but the letter containing the spirit of that advice, as well as several others Williams wrote during the war, were important to the change he made between his first and second books. Some indication of that change may be measured by "The Minimal," a poem Roethke placed in the middle of *The Lost Son* (1948), but finished before May 1942, well in advance of the title piece. In finding a subject attuned to his childhood memories, Roethke had begun to validate an experience different from most of the poems in *Open House*. Roethke sent his poem to Williams (along with two others not identified in Roethke's letters) in the late summer of 1942:

> I study the lives on a leaf: the little
> Sleepers, numb nudgers in cold dimensions,
> Beetles in caves, newts, stone-deaf fishes,
> Lice tethered to long limp subterranean weeds,
> Squirmers in bogs,
> And bacterial creepers
> Wriggling through wounds
> Like elvers in ponds,
> Their wan mouths kissing the warm sutures,
> Cleaning and caressing
> Creeping and healing.[14]

As these examples go, the poem is an able illustration of "no ideas but in things" and suggests that Roethke's interest in Williams's general perspective on poetry had deepened considerably from their first meeting. Williams's response to "The Minimal" does not diminish the poem by claiming it for his side. In his letter of September 22, 1942, he comments in a seemingly offhand way on the larger act behind the voice:

> Of the three poems you enclosed the bug poem pleases me most—the Ancient Mariner watching the slimy things in the red shadow of the ship and blessing them—until finally he could pray. . . .[15]

Brief as it is, Williams bringing the Mariner alongside Roethke's poem offers a rich background for his view of Roethke's development. Williams does not quote the crucial word in Coleridge's description—"And I blessed them *unaware*"—but he clearly emphasizes the spontaneity of the act, suggesting in the comparison that Roethke's poem has gone beyond the prospect of its opening verb to an unstudied recognition of "the less known side." The "slimy things," if we understand them as Williams understood them in "Advice," are a latent comment on the reach of the self ("Give your dragon the words . . .") and on the power of what is commonly avoided to shape a poem. Williams's comparison is, in fact, more enthusiastic than it looks, because the Mariner's blessing had been a prototypically right occasion for scores of his own poems. The stunning "Paterson: Episode 17," already finished in the late thirties, can be read as an extended parallel to the Mariner's blessing, and *Paterson*, Book 1, for all of its steady gaze at the death of spirit, breaks itself free in moments that surprise even the speaker:

> Things, things unmentionable,
> the sink with the waste farina in it and
> lumps of rancid meat, milk-bottle tops: have
> here a tranquility and loveliness
> Have here (in his thoughts)
> a complement tranquil and chaste.[16]

The "things unmentionable," which Williams conspicuously mentions, have their counterpart in the Mariner's water snakes, whose moment of exaltation is followed by tranquility and rain. Roethke would make further use of the moment Williams finds in "The Minimal." In *The Echoing Wood of Theodore Roethke,* Jennijoy LaBelle locates a developing sequence of "slime" images in "The Lost Son" and reads that sequence along the curve of the Mariner's blessing, showing Roethke's personal and literary memories in remarkable congruence. "Like the Mariner, the protagonist in Roethke's poem realizes that the slime contains not only objectionable animal tendencies, but also germs of new possibilities of life, and thus he entreats, 'Snail, snail, glister me forward.' Just as the Mariner finally stops despising the 'thousand, thousand slimy things' and sees their radiance, sees that 'they moved in tracks of shining white, . . . and every track/Was a flash of golden fire,' Roethke sees the slime the snail leaves on its track not as repugnant and viscous but as brilliant substance that 'glisters'— glitters and gleams."[17] Fifteen years later in "The Rose," a poem he especially liked to read, Roethke would clarify his speaker's transcendence with another glance at Coleridge: "And I rejoiced in being what I was / In the lilac change, the white reptilian calm."[18] If the vision in "The Minimal" develops the next phase of Roethke's art, Williams's reading of the poem offers him some part of the literary self he could—and did—become.

Roethke published "The Minimal" in the November 1942 issue of *Harper's Bazaar* with a biographical note reporting that his first book had been praised by Auden, Elizabeth Drew, and Yvor Winters and that his cooking had been praised by Williams: "but Mr. Roethke apparently derives the keenest pleasure from an accolade by William Carlos Williams who dubbed him 'as good a steak cook as Brancusi.'"[19] Aside from the fact that Williams hadn't matched the notice of Auden and the others for *Open House*, Roethke saw an opportunity to publicize another of his skills and to capture Williams and Brancusi for his reputation. The note must have caused him to reflect on his standing with Williams because soon after, possibly on the same day he saw the poem in *Harper's Bazaar*, Roethke wrote to Williams asking his indulgence for using the quote and sending two more poems, "Pickle Belt" ("The factory one will amuse you, I hope") and in all probability "Judge Not," the poem Roethke hoped Williams would take seriously. Although we do not have a record of Williams's response to "Judge Not," the letter interests for the kind of question Roethke thought important to ask and for the story that accompanies the poem:

Look: answer me truly: Has this one about death got the true indignation? It seemed to write itself and by God I mean it. I hope very much you'll like it, but if you don't say so. You're my toughest mentor.[20]

Roethke is building upon Williams's image of what he can become. "It seemed to write itself . . ." records the genesis of the poem; when addressed to Williams, however, it also records Roethke's memory of a sudden, successful raid on "the less known side." (Roethke also sent the poem to Stanley Kunitz late in 1942 with no mention of its seeming to write itself.)[21] Questions about the vitality of language when the mind has lost sight of its ground will persist in Roethke's correspondence, yet the poem is presented as some sort of triumph, a product of forces, themselves coherent, beyond his control:

Judge Not

Faces greying faster than loam-crumbs on a harrow;
Children, their bellies swollen like blown-up paper bags,
Their eyes, rich as plums, staring from newsprint,—
These images haunted me noon and midnight.
I imagined the unborn, starving in wombs, curling;
I asked: May the blessings of life, O Lord, descend on the living.

Yet when I heard the drunkards howling,
Smelled the carrion at entrances,
Saw women, their eyelids like little rags,
I said: On all these, Death, with gentleness, come down.[22]

The poem's most effective lines focus on those unacknowledged parts of a world that for Roethke are also the recesses of the self. If we take the title as his final comment, his suspending judgment affirms their claim to be heard. The poem as well reaches towards a discovery within the drama of accumulating detail, but the discovery is complicated by the fact that the imagery makes a statement apart from the apocalyptic wish of the last line: the examples of misery and degradation that Roethke cites do not so clearly oppose each other that our assent to "On all these, Death . . ." becomes inevitable. What is the categorical difference between "Faces greying faster than loam-crumbs on a harrow" and "women, their eyelids like little rags"? Roethke's question about the "true indignation" is first of all a question about the ability of the poem to create a reader who will be persuaded by the difference.

But much more is at stake in Roethke's question. As his poems of the forties will suggest, Roethke could lay exceptional claim on his own past, and at certain moments, his access seems to have no identifiable borders. Williams was clearly fixed in Roethke's mind as one who knew "the true indignation," and it is not difficult to see why. Roethke is reading Williams's first letter of two years before, where he offered Clytemnestra's rage as an example of language transforming everything in its path, including the chorus's shock at Agammemnon's death:

> So he goes down, and the life is bursting out of him—great sprays of blood, and the murderous shower wounds me, dyes me black and I, I revel like the Earth when the spring rains come down, the blessed gifts of god, and the new green spear splits the sheath and rips to birth in glory![23]

Although the final lines of "Judge Not" may seem limp by comparison, Roethke's question suggests the measure by which he wants to be judged. And in a way that he did not know, the poem that "wrote itself" looks forward to the achievement of "The Lost Son." The reluctance of the imagery to illustrate the neat divide between life and death anticipates the back and forth movement, the ambiguous evocations of his major poems. In "Judge Not" Roethke encounters those indestructible, parabolic faces at the edge of knowing, and his question asks Williams to verify a tone he cannot place. That he would ask the question at all suggests he is willing to try the ground he believed Williams had already crossed. It is a special compliment.

2

"These are the best things of yours . . ."

Roethke's question about the true indignation was indeed much larger than it seemed. It involved an encounter with all of those forms of confinement—social, literary, and often distinctly personal—that inhibit the energies of language. Williams had, in fact, already provided the substance of an answer by referring him to Clytemnestra's speech. What astonished Williams about her speech is the imagery of self-erasure and renewal uncompromised by any hesitation in her voice. Agammemnon's blood falling on her dyes her "black," surely a word that holds within its power connotations of guilt, but releases into the sentence all of the possibilities of fertility and germination that her comparison to earth will supply. Her whole speech centers upon the paradox of "taking in" and "pouring out," as if these transformations opened the earth's secret. The persuasive energy of Clytemnestra's speech, Williams is saying, comes from her identifying with both sides of the paradox, no matter what may happen to the stability of the self. And Roethke, in his notebooks, understood it. Even as he asked the question, he was allowing his turbulent, unaccommodated side to speak in ways more liberal than Williams—or anyone else—imagined. "All My Lights Go Dark," David Wagoner's selection from Roethke's notebooks (1943–47), shows us a poet who is reaching back and starting over, discovering at once a personal history and the multiplied resources of language.[1] Metaphor as magic, incantatory syntax, oracular questions, paradoxes, quips, and satires fill out Roethke's private record; clearly, he is establishing a more spacious personality than the voice of *Open House* announced. With a phrase he would use in writing to Williams and others, Roethke called this the whole process of "loosening up,"[2] and it is a phrase which almost all of the notebook entries quoted by Wagoner define. Roethke wants, as he says, to "make the language take really desperate jumps," to write "a poem that is the shape of the psyche itself."[3] In a host of voices, he would pursue this shape for the rest of his life.

The word "shape" in Roethke's vocabulary carries meanings of "something cut out," and his preoccupation with shape during the years of the war was more central than the variant title for his second book, "The Shape of the Fire," suggests. Poems such as "Cuttings" and "Cuttings (later)" offer a record of involvement and drama that he could not satisfactorily explain. Led by dreams of the greenhouse to recover his earliest memories, Roethke increasingly identified the growth of the self with the buried life of plants, their strategies claiming his voice in unpredictable ways. The two "Cuttings" poems now so easily trace the arc of Roethke's development that they appear to be the products of someone who has understood his direction. When Roethke showed them to Williams in July 1944, however, they were as tentatively offered as the cuttings they describe:

Cuttings

Sticks-in-a drowse droop over sugary loam,
Their intricate stem-fur dries;
But still the delicate slips keep coaxing up water;
The small cells bulge;

One nub of growth
Nudges a sand-crumb loose,
Pokes through a musty sheath
Its pale tendrilous horn.

Cuttings
(later)

This urge, wrestle, resurrection of dry sticks,
Cut stems, struggling to put down feet,
What saint strained so much,
Rose on such lopped limbs to a new life?

I can hear, underground, that sucking and sobbing,
In my veins, in my bones I feel it,—
The small waters seeping upward,
The tight grains parting at last.
When sprouts break out,

> Slippery as fish,
> I quail, lean to beginnings, sheath-wet.[4]

Part of the achievement of both poems lies in the leap between the stanzas. In "Cuttings" the second stanza resolves the paradox of the first by focusing on a "nub of growth" that lives beyond contradiction in an entirely unself-conscious way. In the absence of speech, the speaker's "less known side" fills in the image of its own growth, the willingness to believe in a life so small in its workings and so large in the mystery of its work that it resists a merely reasonable first thought. "Cuttings (later)" makes the whole process more explicit. In the silence that follows the question of verse one, the speaker crosses the border between world and self, proposing at once the carnal, unvoiced language of cuttings for the beginnings of his own "shape." As the second verse doubles the activity of growth with the movements of the "I," the cuttings become "something cut out," and the final version of the self emerges within the event of its own identifications. These exchanges would have been especially alive to Williams, who in poems such as "The Yachts" moves so powerfully from sight to vision that the shift in language has the force of an invasion.

In April 1943, Roethke moved from Penn State to Bennington and met Kenneth Burke, "a good guy of the verbose Irish type," as he would say to Allan Seager.[5] Burke had known Williams since the 1920s and had become, by Williams's own account in the *Autobiography*, one of those irreducible voices that set his poems in motion.[6] Williams's name undoubtedly came up in an early conversation between Roethke and Burke; probably at the urging of both, Williams was invited to give a "talk" at Bennington on June 30, 1944. Although no record of the talk has been preserved, the engagements of Williams's mind can be understood from his letters and the general account of the trip itself.[7] Bennington was one stop on a three-week vacation that he and his wife had planned, a trip on which he brought a copy of *Finnegans Wake* and the materials for *Paterson*, intending to further the relationships among man, city, and falls. Clearly, it was a time to expand. Whatever *Finnegans Wake* may have meant for specific passages in *Paterson*, Williams's reading of it gave him the assurance that his most radical thoughts about form were paralleled by Joyce's inventions in language. At its best, the trip went beyond his expectations in the sudden reach of conversation with strangers. As he said to Roethke, he'd "nearly forgot what Chaucer found on his way to Canterbury, that people are delightful when on a journey, foot-loose and therefore voluble."[8] And the paradox of releasing him-self from the environment of Paterson while confronting its history in poetry and prose gave him that sense of the work as a succession of durable moments, each one contributing to a larger, unfolding, recurrent pattern. Involuntarily, he too had become "footloose" and "voluble," as large as his poem. Near the end of his vacation, he could write to Horace Gregory that he was "steadily aligning the mass of material I had collected for *Paterson* until now all is in order for the first draught."[9]

When Williams met Roethke at Bennington in 1944, then, both poets were discovering the range and design of those poems that would define their careers. Williams's reputation was better estab-lished, and the sustained effort that would bend the language in his direction—and away from Eliot—was at hand. His confidence in the assimilations of *Paterson*, in tracing the giant from the pat-tern of his steps, backgrounds his relationship to Roethke, and his willingness to consider Roethke's new poems in an extended way comes from that one resource he rarely possessed: time. "There could never be a better time for reading them than now," he wrote to Roethke two days after the Bennington talk.[10] Roethke responded immediately, sending at least four poems—the two "Cuttings" pieces, "The Return," and "Visitation"—and inquir-ing whether Williams could be a resident at Bennington for a year. The letter that Williams wrote back, full of encouragement without yielding an inch, depends for its effect not only on the perspicacity of the comment, but on the way it was received. For Roethke, it became a sacred object:

These are the best things of yours that I've seen. Some of them are distinguished, you've emerged to a full and characteristic expression; they are good but they are, more important, you end with distinction as I have said. It is the search for this distinctive, thoroughly mastered, full tone—a 'cello note, one of the lower strings but near its upper register—that at your best makes you ONE, a member of the orchestra, that you are approaching.

That's a pretty flowery first paragraph, but it's not an unconsidered statement. I begin to see you separate yourself from the others, it's a tough upgrade. Here you appear as an an entity. You've mastered the words and the form (not so well as the words but what the hell, who has?) You've shaken off a constraint in the form. Now it's the concentration on the distinctive, the YOU that must follow. I'm keeping the poems and shall read them again later and several times then, possibly, write you again.

Specifically, by all means keep both the poems "Cuttings" in the group, they are both among your best and each, at the same time, has its own excellence. That's where you still have some trouble, an unwillingness to risk putting too much of a thing, of a situation before a reader. It comes of a natural unwillingness to offend by over-statement—but hell, what the Hell difference does it make to YOU so long as YOU see an emphasis, a different aspect of the object, a needed variant of the stress. You've got to have more confidence in the willingness of the reader to be led. He WANTS you to stress, to point, to repeat where necessary to clear the point you are making.

The thing sought is the essence and for this we need release in our technical and emotional resources, we need security, confidence in the need to be saying (as poets!) what we are saying. But in releasing ourselves, in that feeling of confident release the difficulty is that we say too much, we say more than is distinctively ourselves, we slop over a little. It is the usual dilemma. Particularly I'd omit Visitation—it's too God damned like masturbation. I don't like it. Whereas the next poem Return is hard as nails without being hard technically and one of the best.

You suggest Stephens with an important difference of closer knit reasoning, less brick-a-brack and bitter ironic note, almost a sardonic note—framing a much greater tenderness than Stephens ever knew. That's where your difficulty lies, you do not dare to be tender, you fear it. Well, you'd better fear it but to your credit, your great contribution to modern poetry may well be that you have found or are finding a way to express that generosity of spirit in a polished steel mesh or frame that can and must hold it against injury. If you can continue to make poems a long that line, as you have shown you can do in this batch of poems, there is no reason why you should not become one of the most distinguished poets of the day. I think here and there you have already done the trick.

The obligation before you is to continue to write with an increasing lack of self consciousness—because of your fear of yourself as a great big sloppy looking son-of-a-bitch whom a bastard like Untermeyer can smear with a quip so that you have to get drunk to recover from it—with the full warmth and breadth of feeling which is yourself caught in a stell mesh so God damned abrasive, so indestructible that it gives you the only security an artist can ever feel—that in his art lies his only protection.[11]

The abundant praise of Williams's opening paragraph, the first to Roethke after four years of correspondence, was by no means "unconsidered." Williams typically defended his own best work as a rebellion against the herd, and he cultivated, as he knew, exactly the kind of intelligence that Plato would never have allowed inside the gates of his city. With this background, Williams's saying, "I begin to see you separate yourself from the others," becomes something more than encouragement: it represents a value shared and a welcome to the company of outsiders. It also suggests the kind of situation Williams commonly described himself. From "Spring and All" to "Asphodel, That Greeny Flower," Williams involved himself in the struggle of growth and, more precisely, with the point at which things, often startlingly, take on a distinctive shape. "I must tell you/this young tree," the opening lines of "Young Sycamore," tell not only of the necessity of speaking out, but of the suddenly distinguishable entity before us all. For its first-time readers, *Paterson* offers a series of discoveries, won by exclamation points, capitals, and unexpected line breaks from what would surely be Paterson's shadowy and unexciting past if written by a conventional observer. A constituent voice of *Paterson* is, in fact, the voice of someone rescuing "things" from their unmarked graves. In this context, "Say it, no ideas but in things" is still a remarkable statement, not only for the magnitude of its exclusions, but for its commitment to finding meanings in places where they have not been established.

Williams's willingness to find meaning in these new poems was especially welcome to Roethke, who in 1944 was not having the kind of success he had come to expect from the reception of his first book. What Roethke came to appreciate in Williams's letter, however, was something less tangible, which became available only when his skill in discovering the borders of his art made the meanings clear. Interspersed with his comments on Roethke's poems, Williams concerns himself with the poem Roethke has not written, and his attitude is more strongly established than the casual syntax of the letter suggests. From their first meeting, Williams had located a defensive posture in Roethke's work that stopped individual poems short of their larger resolutions. In an early letter, he did not hesitate to call this "form," meaning Roethke's use of traditional structures such as the ballad that confirmed a "stable social order" beyond whatever radical statement that might hold.[12] In this letter, however, he locates it differently— in Roethke's fragile "less known side," where the image of the self asserts its control in the most immediately gratifying way. Williams's illustration is Roethke's drunkenness in the face of Untermeyer's remark, but there is a better example in the letter, an example with implications for Roethke's work that both of them would have understood. It is the poem "Visitation," included with other poems which Roethke wanted Williams to read:

> What gliding shape
> Beckoning through halls
> Stood poised on the stair,
> Fell dreamily down?
>
> From the mouths of jugs
> Perched on many shelves,
> I saw substance flowing
> That cold morning.
>
> Like a slither of eels
> That watery cheek
> As my tongue kissed
> My lips awake.[13]

In his bristling armory of dismissals, Williams's comparing this poem to masturbation has its own distinctive place; it is certainly a comment he thought Roethke would not dismiss. Compared with the two "Cuttings" pieces and "The Return," poems in which the reader is asked to engage the energy of another life, "Visitation" does in fact stand out as a relatively thin and self-congratulatory event. Under the best conditions, the last word, "awake," could extend the life of the poem, but here it abruptly takes back whatever the poem has summoned. "I wake to sleep, and take my waking slow," the first line of Roethke's well-known villanelle, might have been written to restore what the last line of "Visitation" misses.[14] Over the course of his career, Roethke revised at length, often by allowing a later poem to finish what an earlier had begun. Williams already had some evidence of this with the two "Cuttings" poems before him.

Williams's preference for both of those poems, his resistance to the conclusion of "Visitation," and his critical emphasis on the self-limiting boundaries of understatement in Roethke's work suggest what he probably had already said to Roethke in conversation: that longer, more open forms would allow full range to those feelings now only partially realized in the text. At least this is what Roethke would remember. Four years after the Bennington meeting, when he found it necessary to describe Williams's special contribution to his development, he recalled Williams's "jibing me in conversation and by letter to get out of small forms," and he would add, in a statement more than casually revealing, that he inherited his rhythms not from Williams, but from "Mother Goose & Skelton (maybe Blake in his epigrams)."[15] Roethke's acknowledgment of a debt to Williams on this occasion is in itself surprising, since he was defending himself against Selden Rodman's observation that his style "derived from Williams."[16] The larger point, however, is that Roethke's experiments with longer forms were prompted by Williams, by Kenneth Burke, and probably by Allan Seager;[17] he also allowed his language to abandon the task of the sentence, to experience its growth—an effect comparable to life in a greenhouse. In this state, every object, no matter how stunted or ingrown, has a claim on the space it inhabits: one of the better illustrations of this tendency is "The Lost Son," whose fragments were in Roethke's notebooks as early as 1943.[18] Here, the passion for recovering the past—and for inventing the terms that will dramatize its value—is ostensibly spurred by reflections of its loss. So little is "lost" in the "The Lost Son," however, that Williams must have been surprised at what was saved. Not only does Roethke record the prodigal energy, the colliding images and distortions of childhood; he also revives a language that had been apparently "lost," including one sequence of lines which Williams thought had been permanently buried. In Part III of "The Lost Son," Roethke brings back three stanzas of the poem Williams knew as "Visitation," stanzas now embedded in a large—and largely unstated—series of relationships. In effect, Roethke turns "Visitation" back into a fragment, letting the body of the poem speak without the burden of a title or a last line that pretends to conclude the experience. The questions that follow—"Is this the storm's heart? . . . Do the bones cast out their fire?"—suggest that all answers are clear only as the entire action of the poem makes them clear."[19] In its length, its deferral of an immediately satisfying order, its pursuit of the luminous event and its trust of "the less known side," "The Lost Son" assimilates several directions of Williams's criticism and makes of them an object which Williams could barely have foreseen from the work in front of him in June 1944.

"The only reason I haven't written sooner is that I was afraid I would overwhelm you with gratitude, like a St. Bernard," Roethke wrote to Williams in the late fall of 1944. "In fact, I carried the letter around for a time: something to hold against the world."[20] The "world," in this case, was centered in the opinions of John Crowe Ransom and the editors of *Poetry*, who had just rejected several of the same poems that Williams had praised. As with most poets whose work has been turned down, Roethke could describe the forces that opposed him with exceptional facility. "I do think the conceptual boys are too much in the saddle: anything observed or simple or sensuous or personal is suspect right now. Anything with images equals Imagism equals Old Hat."[21] Although Ransom himself could hardly be reduced to the size he is given in Roethke's phrase "conceptual boys," there is enough evidence in his choices for the *Kenyon Review* in 1944 to suggest that Roethke had grasped the principle that excluded him. As an example of the kind of poem that Roethke's work was measured against, Allen Tate's "Seasons of Soul," the first poem in the 1944 volume of the *Kenyon Review*, invites the reader to participate in its symmetries: four sections, four seasons, four elements, rhyme made emphatic by the brevity of the trimeter line, and a repeated last word in each of six stanzas that make up the sections.[22] Within the boundaries it sets for itself, it is a faultless performance: witty, continuously surprising in the latitude of its reference, unrelenting in the kind of equations it proposes for states of soul, the elements and the seasons. The design is explored with exceptional and thoroughgoing assurance. Placed next to "Seasons of Soul," Roethke's greenhouse poems, which Ransom read in the middle of 1944, must have looked not just simple and sensuous and personal but partial, slight, abrupt, broken. Whether Roethke quite realized this or not, the tone of resignation in his letter to Williams ("Oh well, you know all that. . . . ,") asks for some kind of personal reassurance, or at least for agreement that the language characterizing the difference has been rightly understood. And his language does hold some unacknowledged meanings. Below Roethke's phrase, "conceptual boys" lies Emerson's "things are in the saddle . . . ," and if that sentence is allowed its full weight, then Roethke is distinguishing between a poetry that is spiritless, limited, and fully resolved, and one that renews itself by those ranges of association grouped around the surprises of the earth. In the greenhouse poems, Roethke was clearly alive to those surprises, and it is paradoxically true that he needed rejection as a means of keeping himself close to the source of his imagined birth as a flower or a tree. It is also clear that several of the greenhouse poems enact the drama of survival, and it may be that Roethke, who was often his own best analyst, mentioned these rejections as a way of preserving the opposition which he knew would elicit a further response. The speculations are endless, but then with Roethke, so are the impulses that provoke them. He may have wanted Williams to invent praises he had not yet heard.

Williams, of course, could not be predicted. He was obviously capable of bringing several private histories to bear on the problem of the *Kenyon Review*, but when he read Roethke's letters, he customarily resisted all kinds of pressures—here the pressure to become merely stoical and forbearing. If Roethke expected a letter that recommended patience, he had not read Williams closely enough. In his reply, all the more radical because it encourages Roethke to persist with the kind of poem that had failed to interest Ransom, Williams begins by offering a caricature that separates the vitality of children—Roethke and himself—from the mentality of "them Taters." What is remarkable about this letter is that it never rests in the comforts of an imagined reward. In effect, it asks the fool to continue his folly without promising him wisdom—or, if there is wisdom to be had, it may be the kind of wisdom that will cost him his job at Bennington. For the risks it asks Roethke to take, for its announcement of a journey that may be lifelong and for its prescience in urging Roethke to confront the meanings of the greenhouse, this letter is one of the best that Williams ever wrote:

> Serves you right for trying to play around with the Taters. Couldn't you just feel how proud, righteous and uppity they are? Po' chil'un like us ain't for them people from the big house. Now don't you never go where they are again. You hear?
>
> I can see what you mean about imagism as a reason for their not wanting to print you, if this is true. A poem, for them, as you suggest, must have a modern concept as a core before it can be used. Of course they're right but it doesn't have to be dry bone. But they have swallowed the Eliot bait at last (much disguised of course) and from now on poetry, like the owl, will have no serviceable ass hole.
>
> You can't of course, go on developing the hot-house image indefinitely without facing it finally and the result in that case ain't for anybody teaching in a female seminary. As far as I can see the point for you would be to beat those philosophic punks to it by driving your sensuality to an extreme. It can't be done, as I have said, while you are teaching. Then you'll have to give up teaching—but write as you are writing but more so. Make it drunker, hotter, drippier, more unashamed and truer to an adult memory, truer to actual love, to whatever the hell you want to call it.
>
> I'll be looking for the Gugg material but I warn you I'm poison to them guys. Better look for someone else to back you, someone in collegiate circles would have more influence, much more influence than I.
>
> What the various magazines find against you is no doubt what you yourself suggest, a definite—or lack of a definite intellectual concept

about which to correlate your images. You are not definite enough as to what the greenhouse means to you as an overall idea. And you must relate the images, finally, if the full significance is to be seized. Try the Quarterly Review of Literature at Chapel Hill. A man named T. Weiss operates it, he is a damned good critic.[23]

Wallace Stevens' comment on *In the American Grain*, "What Columbus discovered is nothing to what Williams is looking for,"[24] is particularly apt here because Williams is recommending the exploration of a continent beyond that which Ransom and Tate have discovered. In fact, the Williams of *In the American Grain* distinguishes between two kinds of explorers, figures that lend a special energy to this letter. The first, who often acts more as the barely conscious purveyor of a tradition than as an individual, always begins by holding something back: robust, curious, sincere, he is incapable of understanding the promise because he brings a latent model of civilization to the discovery. With this principle, Williams finds unexpected similarities among Cortez, the Columbus of the later voyages, Cotton Mather, Hamilton, Franklin, and Washington. The second kind of explorer, whose story disappears from narrowly official histories, represents the ground of a natively "American" character. He is true to the discovery in the only way Williams considers important: he allows it to change him so radically that he can never return to the self-limiting conventions of the society he has left behind. Like Daniel Boone, he chooses to live miles beyond the edge of civilization, knowing that the wilderness alone has the power to define him; like Sebastian Rasles, he recognizes the superiority of a language that has grown up inside the environment it presents; like Aaron Burr, he is misunderstood by his mostly unadventurous contemporaries.[25] Not directly stated, this distinction nevertheless contributes to Williams's encouragement in the letter to Roethke, and it divides the predictable gestures of "them Taters" from the poet Roethke might become.

It also suggests that Williams, along with his encouragement, is issuing both an immediate and an ultimate challenge, as if he had suddenly met that part of himself that could never be satisfied with enclosures. To invent a "concept" is to engage the

Kenyon Review right at the point of "Seasons of Soul." But this reasonable advice is not at all reasonable if we allow Williams's letter its full range. In asking Roethke to confront the greenhouse, Williams is asking him to go beyond it, to test that meaning with a language that is more sensuous, energetic, and threatening than anything he had yet seen. Clearly, language here is not a way of civilizing the wilderness, but is the wilderness itself explored by something as mysteriously composed as the poem. Although Williams's advice can be as immediately useful as a prescription ("Try T. Weiss . . ."), the voice that addresses Roethke's future is as radical as any that speaks through *In the American Grain.* Without sounding capricious, Williams dismantles the houses in Roethke's letter, and in effect he asks Roethke to do the same. Neither the "big house," with its modernist appearance and antebellum heritage, nor the greenhouse, still incomplete because it has not been "faced," is enough to satisfy him. The only house left is the one not yet built. It is Roethke's next poem.

3

"The Lost Son" and "Russia"

OUT OF THE CAMARADERIE THAT HAD DEVELOPED BETWEEN THEM, Williams might have expected an immediate response from Roethke, but the simple truth is that he had written an unanswerable letter. It asks for risks in language Roethke had not yet taken and for the initiatives of a "modern concept" that can sustain a longer poem. Exactly what Williams means by a "modern concept" is never made clear in the paragraph that introduces the phrase, although his remarkable deference to Tate and Ransom ("Of course they are right . . .") reminds us that *Paterson* is balanced on the equivalences of man and city, language and falls, and that these equivalences act as a silent guide to the important turns in the poem. Whether such a concept would strike Roethke as modern is certainly arguable, but then Williams is less interested in arguing for it than showing the necessity of some sort of design for the reader's continued engagement with the poem. Even Eliot is marshaled into the service of this idea, as if no one, not even the most reluctant of conscripts, could evade Williams's point. Once called up, however, Eliot proves to be an obstinate presence. Certainly the most quotable advice in the letter—"Make it drunker, hotter, drippier . . ."—stands directly opposed to Williams's characterization of Eliot's legacy as "dry-bone." In fact, whatever is unanswerable in this letter is spurred by Williams's reaction to Eliot, who was, in 1944, still unanswered by anybody.

Roethke clearly read all of Williams's letter, including its silences. He also read its challenge, both friendly and intimidating, that no answer would be adequate except by way of the poem. When he did reply, over a year later, it was with a sense of something "found," a poem written to the dimensions of Williams's

41

perspective, and certainly as much as any letter he ever sent, this letter acts as the forerunner of the work. It announces, that is, an event it can hardly contain, the long poem and the Roethke capable of sustaining the long poem, an arrival and the record of a journey:

> But here's a long one which I think is the best I've done so far. It's written, as you'll see right away, for the ear and not the eye. It's written to be heard. And if you don't think it's got the accent of native American speech, your name ain't W. C. Williams, I say belligerently. In a sense, it's your poem—yours and K. Burke's. He's been enthusiastic about it even in its early version. My real point, I suppose, is that I'm not doing one of these but several: with the mood or the action on the page, not talked-about, not the meditative, T. S. Eliot kind of thing.[1]

The open, revelatory style of this letter suggests that nothing is being withheld, but Roethke's silence about the title of the poem—"The Lost Son"—makes its own dramatic statement. Against the background of a sentence such as, "In a sense, it's your poem—yours and K. Burke's," what else could Williams have read except Roethke's claiming him as a kind of father, whose spirit and example have led the "son" into a special way of using language? In the phrase "written to be heard," Williams could bring back not only the history of his readings but the description of his work first given to Roethke six years before: "to listen to the language as it may reveal itself: no line less native to the ear than he's heard spoken." And the Williams engaged in *Paterson* would appreciate the central paradox of "The Lost Son": whatever losses the poem records are being reclaimed in the improvisatory vigor of the language.

Of course it can be said that Roethke's insistence on this point exposes his insecurity about it and that his appeal to Williams's bias for "American" speech is really an attempt to create support for a poem whose future was unsettled. It is true that in the correspondence between Roethke and Kenneth Burke, exchanged during the composition of "The Lost Son," the phrase "native American speech" doesn't appear. Both of them are concerned with the reader's entrance into a long poem without the guidance of external clues. Both of them, that is, are reacting against Eliot's formidable success with private reference and allusion; Burke, as much as Roethke, is interested in keeping the reader's attention on the immediate life of the work. At one point in the early development of "The Lost Son," for example, Roethke sent Burke a draft that included a section Burke will call "Charlie." Burke's advice, and Roethke's acceptance of it, tells us much about the path "The Lost Son" tries to avoid:

> Every once in a while, have read over your verses again. I like the over-all form consid. And many incidental spots. I agree with you that section II needs the most changing. The "Charlie" suffers now from what Police Commissioner Winters would probably call "pseudo-reference." Maybe, experimentally, you should try joycing it (i.e., making up somewhat similar-sounding words at top speed), until you got some further notions as to what content the name had for you; and then you should try to give us this content in imagery more public?[2]

With its casual opening and transference of responsibility to "Police Commissioner Winters," Burke's paragraph nevertheless invokes a principle that would become a serious point for Roethke: the drama of the poem cannot be sustained in teasing but ancillary "plots." The epithet for Winters suggests that Burke is summoning a familiar spirit out of his conversations with Roethke, and certainly a familiar book. In *Primitivism and Decadence*, Winters had explored seven ways of counterfeiting his ideal of "rational coherence" in poetry, and Burke had commented on one of these, "reference to a non-existent plot," in his own *Grammar of Motives*.[3] Both of Winters's examples for this kind of diffusion came from Eliot, a point not lost on Burke when he recommends that Roethke try "joycing" his way out of obscurity. If the manic activity of language, with the sudden recognitions it engenders, can release the self from the obsessive voices of one's own past, it can also, for Burke, rescue "plots" from oblivion. Those voices, committed to the edge of a story the reader can only dimly perceive, compete for attention in the "Charlie" draft:

Yes he did. He stole
He stole for a whole year. Out of the till.

>So he blew blew blew
>So he blew blew blew
>So he blew blew blew
>>off his head,
>>Charlie did.

She went to the book, she did,
Now she's got it all
She went to the book, she did,
She and her Steve.
She went to the book and found what he took
I'd have heated them both
Then she hid the big book, she did
Only mama said No
But I'll break her down
Pay them off some other way
I know how
>>I will I will I will   I
>>will I will I will   I
>>will i will i will i will i   I
>WILL

Ho Charlie ha Charlie ha ha ha Charlie

He's got a hole in his head
Yes he did. I tell you he did.
He stole.

>He knew Schiller though.
>Once a thorn poisoned his green thumb.
>A black rose-thorn.[4]

Behind the drumbeat and roar of these phrasings, there is indeed
a story, one that records a significant change in the Roethke family
history. In the early twenties, Charles Roethke, Roethke's uncle
and a partner in the greenhouse, had been caught altering the
accounts, keeping part of the money for himself and loaning another part back to the company at 6% interest. His embezzling
had brought a series of family quarrels to a crisis and was finally
responsible for the greenhouse being sold. Charles Roethke killed

himself months after the sale; within a year, Otto Roethke, Roethke's father, "in many ways a truly great man" his son would say of him, died of abdominal cancer.[5] Whether Burke knew all of the details or not, this is the story Roethke had to wrestle with: not just the loss of his father, but the loss of his "place" through a series of events he could not control. Burke could propose that Roethke confront the meanings of a name, but for Roethke the consequences were overwhelming. They involve a form of betrayal by someone so close he carries the family name, the loss of a nurturing world, and the encounter with death as a violent, self-imposed act.

The "Charlie" draft shows Roethke assembling a host of voices loud enough to counter the sense of loss and an analogue from German letters large enough to contain it. The voices themselves, whether they appear as machinelike assertions of the self or divinely removed laughter, are caught exercising their first moment of power, as if they were blurting out what the speaker can only record. For most of the passage, they are meant to offer the electrical responses of a child and then with second sight, to distance those responses through the scholar's wisdom. In spite of the experimental appeal of the opening lines, the transformation of voice from the percussive repetitions of "I will I will I will" to a subdued armchair mediation is so problematic that whatever credibility the speaker can rescue almost disappears before the end. Burke's genial complaint about the lack of verbal display and the story that remains private is also a complaint about the readers' position in the final three lines: they are suspended, that is, between a splintered action and an allusion they must complete from their own learning. Most likely, "he knew Schiller" refers to *The Robbers*, where one brother cheats another out of the family estate and intends to kill him. When a sudden reversal makes him face his crimes, he takes his own life. Not surprisingly, the favorite flower of both brothers is the rose, and while the suicide is differently managed in *The Robbers*, the phrase "blow it away with the breath of my lips" appears as a kind of motif in the malevolent brother's last rant.[6] The final effect of the "Charlie" passage depends on readers recovering the parallels and satisfying themselves that the boundaries of life are circumscribed by art. Just when they thought they were marooned by unanswered questions concerning the meaning of Charlie's act, they have been given a clue. The footprint in the sand belongs to Franz von Moor.

Though Burke does not quite put it this way, ideal readers for these lines are the ones turned out by a generation of Eliot scholarship—readers who match their wits with the text, ponder an allusion, and confirm their discovery within the institution of literature. In a sense they have "joined a church," an *ecclesia*, an assembly of called-out ones. Whether Eliot wanted this is difficult to say—his embarrassment over the notes to "The Waste Land" suggests that he did not—yet his finding them irreplaceable shows how submissive he was to the history of the poem. Burke's attempt to return Roethke to the sounds of words is an attempt to counter the deadening repetitions, the hermetic laughter, and the self-protecting allusions of the "Charlie" passage with a series of accidents that will drive him out of his comfortable accommodations. The self, Burke is saying, can only be found by first being lost, and lost in an unexpected way: in the play, the suspensions, the wilderness of language where words themselves hold the manic power to shape a discovery. Burke does not often reify language, but his emphasis on the word-as-act naturally leads him to stress the evocative over the instrumental; he is well on his way to saying that words can be creatively regarded as titles of books, whose pages fill out character, situation, and drift.[7] Like Williams, he could give pointed advice, and to a mind as adventurous as Roethke's, the prospect of "joycing" would have been attractive. Although no record of Roethke's performing this exercise appears in the drafts of "The Lost Son," we know that he liked not only to startle his thought but transform it within the design of the poem. At least one series of lines suggests that he took Burke seriously:

> Dark hollows said, lee to the wind,
> The moon said, back of an eel,
> The salt said, look by the sea,
> Your tears are not enough praise,
> You will find no comfort here,
> In the kingdom of bang and blab.[8]

The potential for rhyming the last syllable of "Charlie" with "lee," "sea," and "eel," and the first syllable with "dark," "said," and "salt" argues for the kind of "joycing" that went on. Even a line such as "In the kingdom of bang and blab," which depends for its effect on the sounds already established in the stanza, may have arisen this way; it brings with it a special, ominous meaning when read against the background of the "Charlie" episode. The larger point, however, is what Roethke made of it and what task readers are asked to perform. What Roethke achieved are lines that focus on the duplicitous character of existence itself: the sense of being thrown into the world where one has been acted upon before one can act; where the desire for wholeness is continually betrayed by attempts to achieve it; where estrangement and the possibilities of transcendence are nevertheless mysteriously related. And readers are asked to remain lost in the welter of voices that speak through this part of the poem until they are offered an environment where the apparent coincidences of earth, sky, and self are brought into a fragile, but necessary, relationship.

In ways more immediate than are usually acknowledged, the conflict between lost and found forms the central drama of "The Lost Son," and this drama embodies what Roethke thought he had accomplished with the work. Initially, more appears to be lost. Before they have finished the first section of the poem, readers have met at least five variations on the theme of absence, experienced the difference between an "I" and a discontinuous "me," confronted a series of riddles standing like signs without signposts, allowed a host of voices to remove them from stable narrative ground, and understood that a knowledge of literature will not easily mark their position or bearing. Not even Eliot, with the poem Roethke is writing against, so thoroughly turns his readers over to random and conflicting directions; when he does, such paracletes as Ezekiel, Shakespeare, and Baudelaire arise to keep them within the traditional borders of literature. In "The Lost Son," the gaps, mostly felt in the lack of interpretive comment and precisely measured quotation, act like forms of energy inviting readers to remain lost. Not all of them feel this way, however, partially because the "son" of the title claims for the speaker a close familiar tie, and more subtly, because the forms by which loss is communicated are thoroughly recognizable. Most prominent of these is the riddle, where the drama invests itself in the elusive, magical properties of language. What has four legs but cannot run? From a child's perspective, the answer depends on the power of a single word to pass through the wall separating one meaning from another. Words, indeed, have a "spirit;" they appear without warning and they walk in disguise. This perception of language stands behind the riddles that close the first part of the poem:

> Is it soft like a mouse?
> Can it wrinkle its nose?
> Could it come in the house
> On the tips of its toes?
>
> Take the skin of a cat
> And the back of an eel,
> Then roll them in grease,—
> That's the way it would feel.
>
> It's sleek as an otter
> With wide webby toes
> Just under the water
> It usually goes.[9]

Whatever this is—and we are never told directly—it is simultaneously elusive and close-at-hand. The form concentrates our attention on the power of a word, as well as the supposed existence of a thing, to fulfill the conditions of the search. The word itself, however, never arrives, and Roethke preserves the balance between lost and found in the balance between a tantalizingly full set of clues and the absence of an answer. At this point in the poem one of the speaker's voices trusts the shapes language can assume more than anything it can ultimately represent.

As much as anything else, "The Lost Son" is about language, its ritualized use, its hidden energies, the sudden presence of meaning, its effects and its loss. No better example surfaces in the poem than Roethke's use of the word "Ordnung," an oracular command that announces the coming of "Papa" and becomes a general call to attention.[10] "Ordnung" customarily translates as "order" or "arrangement," but the resonance is far wider, here offering connotations equal to those found in religious communities, where the life of an entire society develops by way of an "order." In the poem, it gathers amplitude from its associations with the father, with the roses and with light, and it appears just at the point when the desire for abandonment, brought forward in the unanswered questions and the surreal accumulations of imagery, seems bound to prevail. It is also spoken in the greenhouse, that place where the wild is brought indoors and made into a kind of community to emphasize the exotic potential of individual life. For the moment, everything is poised, secure, expectant; the word has been found and it is enough. By the last section of the poem, however, its meaning has all but vanished, and the speaker himself is waiting for a "lively, understandable spirit," a phrase that only vaguely approximates the fullness of everything that has gone before.[11] Although the last lines have a peacefully ruminant air, the emphasis falls on something lost. The last word, "Wait," narrowly misses bringing back all of the unanswered questions by its position in a descending staircase of comforting assertions. In accommodating the loss, "The Lost Son" offers one of the most subdued conclusions in American poetry.

In writing to Williams, however, Roethke avoids commenting on the poem's lengthy involvement with displacement, confusion, and loss. Instead, he presents it as a breakthrough in his own struggles with the long poem, and more, a victory in its capture of the "accent" of American speech. Though Roethke opens a wide speculative horizon in using the word "accent," his point is that the poem should draw its reader by an act of recognition as immediate as the one between two strangers in a foreign country who discover they speak the same language. Whatever their subject, their speech is their bond. In the letter, Roethke all but asks that Williams pass over the poem's accumulation of losses to reach its concealed identity: its spare vocabulary, its punctuated rhythms, its avoidance of lines requiring notes and glosses, its emphasis on the word-as-act. "The Lost Son," as Neal Bowers has recognized, is more than the record of a journey or a state in the recognition of a self; it is an exploration of language caught in the act of performing its exuberantly childlike rituals.[12] Sometimes explainable and sometimes as elusive as "London Bridge," the lines continually surrender the evolution of an argument to the needs of cadence, space, recurrence, babble, and the sudden release of voices. It might be said that "The Lost Son" is a poem where the body astonishes the mind, if mind is understood as the reader's desire for some conventional assurances of the narrator's ability to offer a meaning for every phrase. But the well-controlled vocabulary, following Williams's emphasis on the "native" and the "spoken," makes the hallucinated turns seem familiar even when they hunt the strange. Take, for example, a part of the stanza Roethke may well have "joyced" into existence:

> Dark hollows said, lee to the wind,
> The moon said, back of an eel,
> The salt said, look by the sea . . .

The second line is especially troublesome, and most critics just avoid it. Jay Parini, with the clarity he brings to his overall reading of the poem, faces the problematic symbolism with good sense: "The moon's response cannot be pinned down with any ease. Traditionally, the moon is a feminine principle whereas the eel is likely to be male."[13] From this approach, probably little more can be said. It is important to notice, however, that the moon doesn't tell the narrator to travel any great distance. In effect, it offers an answer in something as common as an eel, and the simplicity of the word suggests the presence of a vocabulary that is unbreakably secure. Bear, moon, sea, mouse, cloud—words such as these discover the world, our early world, in the pleasure of naming. "The Lost Son" is still a poem where one-hundred-fifty monosyllabic nouns appear in a comparable number of lines, where "eel," "stone," and "light" are repetitively enriched throughout the work, and where "understandable" is the longest word readers encounter. "A lively understandable spirit" may well be the spirit of language itself, animating by pitch, tone, and resonance the energy inherent in things. American in the sense of evoking what is commonly found, it moves with the power of a commonly available vocabulary. And it celebrates the first acts by which the world is grasped, even if the world presents itself as shifting and deceptive, controllable mostly in the utterance that gives it form.

With Williams recovering from a herniotomy during the week of May 11 (1946), he and Floss read "The Lost Son," "both looking at the script together."[14] In a handwritten note to Roethke, he replied that the poem had made a strong impression on both of them. For himself, he said:

> I like the poem, three ways: the language, the swing of it and the overall theme. I agree it is your best to date. I am proud to have you say I had something at least to do with it . . . But the best stanza of the poem is the last one, technically—it fades away with the musical quality that is masterful. In the very middle part of the poem the stanzas get a little too slick—know what I mean?—need some such break in the rhythm as you give at the end. *Not* the *same* change of pace but a shade more variable in one place. . . .

> My last blast at Eliot was no more than a word or two in a criticism of a poem by Parker Tyler. . . .[15]

Williams's response to the language of "The Lost Son" touches an old obsession, revived with energy throughout *Paterson* I and especially in the conclusion. There, in the aftermath of a tremor, Mr. Paterson glimpses the source of all language "in that cavern, that profound cleft . . . Earth, the chatterer, father of all / speech."[16] The lines take on a special resonance when read, as I think Williams wanted them read, in the contentious critical world created by "The Waste Land." The "blast against Eliot" Williams announces in his letter to Roethke is a reference to the "sweet blight" of "The Waste Land," and most of his energy in the review comes from reacting against that "catastrophe."[17] A language that is exuberant and uncontrived is always a momentous issue for Williams; his locating the source of it all in the "Earth" suggests that these qualities are as democratically available as the ground. The counter to this is Eliot's view of language in the last section of "The Waste Land." When the thunder speaks, its meanings are twice removed: first in their general inaccessibility to the English-speaking reader and then, when translated, in their Himalayan challenge.[18] The heroic effort to resist the waste of language and enter the future with three Sanskrit words can certainly be admired, yet the fragments at the end of the poem tell us that Eliot's speaker is caught in his own "sweet blight." How resist the corruptions of language except by a language already corrupted? Williams will have his own paradoxes to face in *Paterson,* but his locating the source of language already in "Earth . . . the chatterer" is an act of faith in the renewable energies of speech. His commending Roethke for "the language, the swing of it and the overall theme" is a commentary on Roethke's own trust in the capacity of ordinary language, the "chatter," to sustain alterations of voice, changes of rhythm, and those self-expansions written into the sense of loss.

The private joke in this note becomes accessible when read across the background of Williams's experience with Roethke's work. "In the very middle part of the poem, the stanzas get a little too slick—know what I mean?" refers to Roethke's including the poem Williams knew as "Visitation" as part of the third section. By comparing the poem to masturbation, Williams thought he had sent it into permanent exile, but Roethke may have brought it back precisely for that reason: as another episode in the drama that crosses the border between plenitude and loss. Williams's word for all of this is "slick," a word meant to suggest, along with its usual meanings, that the rhymed and metricized harmonies of "Visitation" are an anxiously simplistic way of bringing it off. What Williams focuses on is the loss of self-consciousness, the "fadeaway" at the end of "The Lost Son," where both "I" and "me" disappear, and the power to create an event is transferred to light, the earth, and a "lively understandable spirit." Although Williams had joined Roethke's success to lack of self-consciousness for at least three years, the conclusion of "The Lost Son" represents the first time Williams had encountered a long passage in Roethke's poems that achieves an intimacy with the world without the pressures of a monitoring ego. In its own way, Williams's reading of this part of the poem is astonishing because it takes the word "lost" further than Roethke intended, or perhaps even understood. When Roethke wrote about the ending of the poem in an essay entitled "Open Letter," he called up a human figure for these lines, as if the poem required some characterological weight to keep its balance:

> In the final untitled section, the illumination, the coming of light suggested at the end of the last passage occurs again, this time to nearly grown man. But the illumination is still only partly apprehended; he is still waiting.[19]

The lines don't require this kind of ballast, however, and Williams's reading concentrates on the transparency that will define Roethke's best moments as a poet in the next decade. For Williams, the whole question of an identifiable speaker isn't an issue at all. As he reads it, the last section has been phased into a record of those shifts in being so charged with life that the speaker is lost in their arrival. When he exists at all, he follows with unhurried amazement the fall of light and a voice assuring him that the world presents itself in cycles of resistance and discovery. Plot, will, search—everything except the voice is casually dispersed at the end.

This, at least, is the poem that Williams read, and it is now possible to see that Burke and Williams, temperamental differences aside for the moment, approached Roethke's work with a similar understanding of their critical role. Both committed themselves to freeing the poem from artifice, self-aggrandizement, and the Eliot-like fascination with difficulty without diminishing the spirit that, in Roethke, seemingly lets language rise from the earth. Burke was far more actively involved with the composition of "The Lost Son," making a decade of his thought available to Roethke through his books, his overflowing talk, and generous letters. Brendan Galvin has shown the remarkable congruity between Burke's analysis of redemption-by-decay, nakedness, incest-awe, and "engrossment," and Roethke's enactment of these themes in the imagery of mildew and slime, ice and fire, roses, bones, and seed.[20] Even the paradox Roethke trusted to give his past collective meaning—"One must go back to go forward"— comes from Burke, as Roethke acknowledged in one of his letters.[21] Burke's contribution to all "The Lost Son" represents may well have come from a different direction, however. Anyone who reads *The Philosophy of Literary Form* has to be impressed by Burke's capacity to elaborate an argument through competing perspectives, aphorisms, verbal coincidences, and imaginative flights combined with dives toward the ground of social talk. His ingenuity can be excited by the freewheeling, auditory power of language itself. In one of his letters to Roethke, for example, he outlines his reading for *A Rhetoric of Motives* against an environment of words fabricated to confront world events in 1945:

> Then, about ten o'clock, I lay aside the Angelic Doctor and take up *Tristram Shandy,* and so gradually to (sleep—to be fit) for the next morning's grind, written with the thought of all that nauseatingly hypocritical and suicidally unimaginative word-slinging, mingendo, cacando, flebotomando, a new consignment of which will reach me when the mail brings the papers at one-thirty.[22]

Burke means this criticism seriously, but the life of the sentence comes from the exuberant comic spurt in the center. Such moments show us the Burke who could shift tones and voices with surprising ease. Denis Donoghue calls him a fox rather than a hedgehog, mostly because Burke is not so overbearingly committed to one idea that readers must give up their identities to follow him.[23] He might be called a fox in his approach to language as well, one fascinated by the uses of cadence, repetition, and sound. In the shaping of "The Lost Son," he was surely as good a critic as Roethke could have hoped for, supporting the overall stylistic experiments the poem finally offers. One of the poem's real accomplishments comes with the compact most readers are willing to make between the child in themselves, the language rituals of childhood, and the "open spaces" inviting wonder and possibility. When Burke first described "The Lost Son" as a "Chronic Throw-back," he was commenting on the poem's ability to expand our awareness of the potential selves within a self, each with a voice and the rudiments of a history.[24]

"In a sense, it's your poem—yours and K. Burke's." Behind that tribute stands the Williams who had involved himself for years with the risks inherent in a "modern concept," with the discovery of an American idiom and the invigorating relationship between lost and found. This last phrase would not have been vague for him. In the history of his correspondence with Roethke, it means all Clytemnestra's rage can represent, a vision so final the language of a world remade transforms any event that precedes it. It can mean the loss of the ordinary, uncommitted self in the magnetism of things, as if each held powers of metaphor that an exactly focused attention could release. And it also means a kind of Apollonian serenity, where the lack of desire is ground for awakening those dream images at the borders of the known. The poem Williams included in his letter to Roethke illustrates these meanings in an unusual way. Entitled "Russia" and published in *The New Republic* two weeks before, it would bring Williams the kind of notoriety he did not want.[25] As evidence for his "Communist" sympathies, it would be read by government officials in the McCarthy era as a political tract, contributing finally to Williams's losing an appointment as Consultant in Poetry at the Library of Congress.[26] When Williams sent it to Roethke, however, he was suggesting a kinship between the narrator's "fadeaway" at the end of "The Lost Son" and the poet's willingness, in "Russia," to be lost in his dream. The quality both poems share is a kind of luminous receptivity, the figure of the speaker vanishing into his aura. Here is the close of "Russia":

> There you have it. It's that background
> from which my dreams have sprung. These
> I dedicate now to you, now when I am
> about to die. I hold back nothing. I lay
> my spirit at your feet and say to you:
> Here I am, a dreamer. I do not
> resist you. Among many others, undistinguished,
> of no moment—I am the background
> upon which you will build your empire.[27]

Flattish and apparently innocent, the voice in these lines is unmistakably Williams, yet the drive toward self-dispersal takes a surprising turn. It is joined to the poem's capacity for moving the reader toward a complex understanding of the word "empire." As it appears here, it is much closer to "promise" or "bond" than the apocalyptic climaxes imagined for it by Communist hunters in the 'forties. "Empire" may not be the most fortunate choice, and it is now easy to see that the poem was accident-prone. Williams's sending it to Roethke along with the note about "The Lost Son" tells us something about his own emphasis, however. It suggests that poems begin in the encounter with some communal or personal resistance: they are not expressions of self; they are attacks on it, quiet but spectacular betrayals. It also brings forward Williams's idea that the poem has an autonomous power capable of directing the speaker into its own courses. On the surface, "Russia" moves between the resistances of a somewhat cranky "poet" and the dream of a shared identity with Russians. A parallel movement is toward finding a voice and language that will persuasively clarify such a dream. The speaker invokes Whitman's voice ("Come with me . . .") and a memory of Mayakovsky, but the poem disposes of them in favor of a wholly different encounter. In the "severity and simplicity" of Leonardo's background for *The Last Supper*, the speaker discovers the origins of his dream, and once found, his life, made interchangeable in the poem with his restlessness, is no longer a necessity. "Russia" is Williams's version of the poet's self-erasure in apparent submission to his dream. More than this, it is his essay on the demands of art, on the transformations made necessary in meeting "the less known side." The "empire" of "Russia," Williams is saying, is the empire of the poem.

4

The Field of Action

WHEN WILLIAMS AND ROETHKE READ EACH OTHER, THEY BROUGHT their present discoveries, their history as poets and the special history of the correspondence to the experience. They read the line in front of them and speculated on its future in the margins. The creative turmoil Roethke knew at the time of "The Lost Son" made everything extraordinarily—and instantly—available. As he would later walk into stores in Seattle and expect to leave with whole counters of merchandise, so lines, tempos, and tones became his possession in 1946 by what he regarded as the impersonal rights of art.[1] Roethke never commented on Williams's "Russia," and the letter he sent back deftly avoids an encounter by stating that he has been reading *another* of Williams's works, *The Wedge*.[2] But some part of "Russia" has been absorbed by "The Long Alley," the poem he included with the letter.[3] As I have suggested, the speaker in "Russia" achieves his final authority by opening the poem to voices and events that will act as convergent energies. One of these is named:

> O Russia! Russians! come with me into
> my dream and let us be lovers,
> connoisseurs, idlers—Come with me
> in the spirit of Walt Whitman's earliest
> poem, let us loaf at our ease—a moment
> at the edge of destruction.[4]

Williams summoning the spirit of Whitman's poem means that he wants to elicit the most liberating kind of response, an awareness that the body's knowledge can open the way to social harmony. The tone is as inviting as Whitman's epigraph to *Leaves of Grass:*

Come, said my Soul,
Such verses for my Body let us write, (for we are one,)
That should I after death invisibly return,
Or, long, long hence, in other spheres,
There to some group of mates the chants resuming,
(Tallying Earth's soil, trees, winds, tumultuous waves,)
Ever with pleas'd smile I may keep on,
Ever and ever yet the verses owning—as, first, I here and now,
Signing for Soul and Body, set to them my name.[5]

At work in these lines is Whitman's challenge to conventional distinctions—body and soul, life and death, time and timelessness—coiled within a syntax that encompasses them all. A half-century before Williams, Whitman understood that a disruptive but compelling language could be found in claiming the soul's unity with the body, along with that larger "body," the earth. "To loafe at our ease" is to bid for this unity. Whitman's unconventional spelling argues for a quite special, mystical activity. Williams doesn't follow the spelling, but he claims Whitman's freedom to translate the body's desires into a political vision: "O Russia! Russians! come with me into / my dream and let us be lovers. . . ." The lines are the boldest move in "Russia," so remarkable in their assurance that they threaten to pale the rest of the poem.

No reader of "Russia" would confuse the relatively stable and trustworthy voice of that poem with the prowling explorations of "The Long Alley." Trying to account for the poet's waywardness even as it is experienced, Williams's perspective contrasts with Roethke's collocations of song, prayer, riddle, question, and plea. "The Long Alley" has been described as a poem about "sexual guilt" and "the acceptance of the erotic experience";[6] a poem where "the son's religious search intensifies, the quest for God and illumination becoming more self-conscious;"[7] a poem focusing on a "purgative cleansing of will;"[8] and a poem "where the hero is not running away from his desires, which is a start in the right direction."[9] Most critics notice a movement from compulsions that bewilder, constrain, and disrupt the speaker to awarenesses that begin to transform and develop him. One of these is so prominent that it is often quoted:

Come littlest, come tenderest,
Come whispering over the small waters,
Reach me rose, sweet one, still moist in the loam,
Come, come out of the shade, the cool ways,
The long alleys of string and stem;
Bend down, small breathers, creepers and winders;
Lean from the tiers and benches,
Cyclamen dripping and lilies.
What fish-ways you have, littlest flowers,
Swaying over the walks, in the watery air,
Drowsing in soft light, petals pulsing."[10]

The excitement of these lines rises from Roethke's perception of the earth's fragility; the inviting tone rests mostly on Williams's reading of Whitman in "Russia." In both poems, the language of love envelopes an unlikely subject, and in both the lines appear just beyond the midpoint, acting like a bend or curve in the speaker's search for the right course. The differences, too, are clear. With surgical precision, Williams lays open the invitation and its source. Roethke's speaker apparently wants to create the garden that will take him in. Or does he? Compared with Williams's "Let us be lovers," Roethke's sentence has no very definite goal. The superlatives, repetitions, and oppositional structures enact the loss of self in the process of creation: even the illusion of a "me" disappears by the end of the stanza. Moments of self-erasure in Roethke can be moments of exceptional clarity, moments of discovery, and at this point in the poem, Roethke is discovering both the relaxed buoyancy of the meditative act and the sense of interconnection given over by the long line. The stanza is made emphatic by its contrast with all that has gone before: the staccatoed assertions with the quietly accumulated energy in a sentence of almost fifty words. Its real attraction, however, comes from an enlivened sense of receptivity, the trait Williams had commended in his reading of "The Lost Son"'s close. Whitman celebrated this mode in section 39 of "Song of Myself" and section three of "Crossing Brooklyn Ferry." Williams, in poems from The Wedge such as "The Clouds," "The Semblables," and "Perfection," certainly knew it. A single aphorism does not answer for all of their work, but it suggests the kind

of self-abandonment all three could persuasively record: "The
greatest traveler does not know where he is going."

Williams does not comment directly on this spirit in "The Long
Alley," mostly because he assumes Roethke will have understood
its importance from his previous letter. Instead, he adopts a tone
the New Critics might have appreciated:

> The poem, to me, is the best yet—in the texture especially; much
> denser, closer packed but not at all obscure because of that. You're
> moving toward a much more complete expression and, indeed, have
> reached it in this piece.[11]

It's clear that Williams is drawing upon Ransom's *The New Criticism* to compliment the "texture" of Roethke's poem; it may be
less clear that he is also drawing upon Kenneth Burke's review of
the limited usefulness of the term as it was first proposed. "Texture," for Ransom, resides in the "details" of a poem and may
comprise "a great deal of irrelevant foreign matter which is clearly
not structural but even obstructive."[12] For Burke, insofar as he
follows Ransom, a poem's texture may be rich and compelling
enough to generate its own inner form. "I think," he says in his
review, "that Mr. Ransom could profitably round out his terminol-
ogy by some such third term as the 'structure of texture.' Studies
like Caroline Spurgeon's *Shakespeare's Imagery*, for instance, or
Lane Cooper's treatment of the fascination theme in Coleridge's
Mystery poems, remind us that the poem does have some principle of organization other than the mere logical structure. . . .
There is a general tenor discernable among the heterogeneities,
something that limits the range of variations, or that points them
thematically in the same direction."[13] As a reader, Williams is
closer to Burke than Ransom in his willingness to give the "textures" voice and shape before he finds the direction that will
bring them together. He is also closer to Burke in his response to
the transformations of language, letting nuance and connotation
create the life of the work. His short paragraph on "The Long
Alley" is remarkable for what it does not do: it does not para-
phrase, does not ask for immediate thematic unity, does not refer
to "structure." Williams has become, in one of Ransom's compari-

sons, "the critic who goes straight from one detail to another, in the manner of a bee who gathers honey from the several blossoms as he comes to them, without noticing the bush which supports the blossoms."[14] To this Williams might have replied: "It is the blossom that intoxicates the bee . . ." And so on. Most of the modernist battle for the reader's eye, ear, tolerance, and attention surfaces in this argument. To read by way of texture is to allow for all kinds of freedoms within the work that a reader in search of structure would find disruptive. It allows for whatever is arbitrary, playful, or discontinuous in the name of a drama that only casually solicits pattern or "order." But the best image for understanding Williams as a reader does not finally correspond to Ransom's bees and blossoms. It is altogether more personal. Williams has become the reader who in the largest sense is ready for a "walk." He is ready, that is, to give himself over to its cadence, to take waywardness and digression as opportunities for exploring the life of language, and to resist the idea of a resolution or climax."[15] The eighty-nine lines of Roethke's poem encourage such a reader, and the "Alley" of the title, with its root in the Latin *ambulare*, asks for an involvement with everything charged by the power of being.

In reading Roethke's "textures," Williams also read his own and probably better than he knew. During the winter of 1946–47 Williams was preoccupied with finding a form for the materials of *Paterson II*, a lot of "loose stuff," as he would say, waiting for the "thread."[16] The problem was both small and large. The large problem centered on a plan for the entire work: no part of it, Williams now felt, could go forward without a much subtler sense of design than the inciting moments of Book I has offered. The more immediate problem involved the ground for Book II. How bring his speaker into a tense, yet intimate relationship with the various languages of Paterson under the form of one dramatic occasion? Williams's solution, as rich in possibility as Mark Twain's taking Huck and Jim down the Mississippi, became Dr. Paterson's Sunday walk up and into Garrett Mountain. Yet Williams is very careful with Dr. Paterson. If he was ever tempted to draft an entire book for a self-scrutinizing voice, it must have been here: Dr. Paterson patrolling the streets like the speaker in "Little

Gidding." That this does not happen bears witness to his genius
for conflating Paterson, the character, with Paterson, the environment. It also makes central his insight into the close of "The
Lost Son:" the poem "fades away with a musical quality that is
masterful."[17] Williams's sensitivity to this effect in Roethke's poem
parallels his way of inventing Dr. Paterson for Book II. Although
Williams meant his speaker to be a continuous presence in Book
I because the events can be construed as his "thought," many
readers feel that he comes and goes. In Book II, however, all the
roles that Williams claims for Dr. Paterson—witness, historian,
poet, storyteller, recipient of letters from an unknown source—
connect with the ground of Paterson through the activity of
"walking":

> Walking—
>
>> Thickets gather about groups of squat sand-pine,
>> all but from bare rock . .
>>
>> —a scattering of man-high cedars (sharp cones),
>> antlered sumac .
>>
>> —roots, for the most part, writhing
>> upon the surface
>>   (so close are we to ruin every
>> day!)
>>   searching the punk-dry rot
>
> Walking—[18]

The present participle keeps everything in balance—and in motion. Like a musical note or riff, it is the beginning and then the
middle of an action that can be completed by any number of
endings: it engages whatever is momentarily resonant and *given*.
In an early and influential review of *Paterson I*, Randall Jarrell saw
how the poem might be apprehended with the analogy of musical
form. "Mr. Williams introduces a theme that stands for an idea,
repeats it over and over in varied forms, develops it side by side
with two or more themes that are being developed, recurs to it
time and time again throughout the poem, and echoes it for ironic
or grotesque effects in thoroughly incongruous contexts."[19] Five
years later, in reviewing Books I–IV and saying that "*Paterson* has

been getting rather steadily worse," he dismissed Book II without letting himself see the measure of Williams's explorations.[20] Between the publication of Book I and the formation of Book II, Williams's interest in jazz surfaced with the writing of poems such as "'Ol Bunk's Band," where the rhythmic energies, as Carol Donley has observed, can be compared to "ostinato figures, syncopations and delayed beats."[21] The comparison can't be worked out with the same precision for Book II, but it points toward the improvisational field Williams wants to enter. In the text, a repeated participle such as "walking" invites the reader to focus on the relationship between action and event without looking back to an agent or even a "subject." Indeed, it suppresses the subject, as if the continuous action it represents had no need of an identifying consciousness. What Williams achieves in the opening section of Book II is closely related to his perception of Roethke's achievement at the close of "The Lost Son." His speaker, and those readers who are willing to follow him, are lost in the venture of becoming what the next moment offers. In the silences that fall between the action of walking and the act of finding the right ground for "Paterson," Williams is exploring the relationship between self-abandonment and identity. And "walking," the signifier of movement, makes the text to follow an emblem of discovery. The energy of *Paterson*, as Jarrell recognized, is the energy of music, but in Book II it is developed more radically and more variously—with more emphasis on change, excitement, and dispersal—than he was willing to allow.

In *I Wanted to Write a Poem* Williams said that he believed Book II a "milestone," emphasizing the discovery of the "variable foot," two-thirds of the way through the book, as the final conception of what his poetry ought to be.[22] He also meant the discovery of the successively indented three-line stanza, a form offering disciplined flexibility for the use of duration, stress, and tempo. Almost all of Williams's poems published in the mid-fifties follow this form. In fact, he liked the lines from Book II so much that he published them again as a single poem, "The Descent," in *The Desert Music* (1954):

> The descent beckons
>   as the ascent beckoned
>   Memory is a kind

of accomplishment
        a sort of renewal
               even
an initiation, since the spaces it opens are new
places
        inhabited by hordes
               heretofore unrealized,
of new kinds—
        since their movements
               are towards new objectives
(even though formerly they were abandoned)

No defeat is made up entirely of defeat—since
the world it opens is always a place
        formerly
               unsuspected. A
world lost,
        a world unsuspected
               beckons to new places
and no whiteness (lost) is so white as the memory
of whiteness .

With evening, love wakens
        though it shadows
               which are alive by reason
of the sun shining—
        grow sleepy now and drop away
               from desire .

Love without shadows stirs now
        beginning to waken
             as night
advances.

The descent
        made up of despairs
               and without accomplishment
realizes a new awakening :
        which is a reversal
of despair.

    For what we cannot accomplish, what
is denied to love,
    what we have lost in the anticipation—
              a descent follows,
endless and indestructible .[23]

The speaker's perspective, both inside and outside the experience, brings another stylistic life to *Paterson*. "The descent beck-

ons" is in one sense remarkable because it does not win its way with experiments in rhyme, with exclamatory outbreaks or with the kind of blocky constructions that are typical of passages around it. The tone of relaxed immediacy seems to remove it from the context of Garrett Mountain, yet the visual form of the passage suggests a sequence of "steps." More, the shuttling of the reader's eye from the "descent" in the triadic stanza back to the left-hand margin excites a sense of renewal. The effect is enhanced by a series of incrementally developed clauses within loose syntactic frames, so the whole reaches for the feeling of ascent. Suggesting an authorial presence apparently beyond the scope of Dr. Paterson, at least in the localized way he has been presented so far, it is a meditation that conveys the subdued but ceaseless activity implicit in the present participle "walking." It is Williams's encounter with the tensions of "one must go back to go forward," where each side of the equation evolves with rhetorical enlargements and rhythmic surprises into a statement of astonishing inner calm.

As a way of suspending moments within a form that asks for movement, exploration, and risk, Williams's discovery of the triadic stanza invites comparison with a Roethke characteristic. Richard Blessing has argued that Roethke's obsession with the primitive energies of being led him to search for forms, including forms of verbs, expressive of ongoing motion and vitality.[24] One of these is the present participle, a verbal drawing past and future into a continuum and conferring a sense of everlasting life on its subject. Roethke used so many of these in the greenhouse poems that the greenhouse itself appears to live within their unfolding, outside the diminishments of time. The Roethke poems Williams admired while he was beginning work on *Paterson II* display a special relationship to this world of quiet persistence. Following are the opening lines of "The Lost Son" (V) and "The Long Alley":

> It was beginning winter,
> An in-between time,
> The landscape still partly brown:
> The bones of weeds kept swinging in the wind,
> Above the blue snow.

It was beginning winter,
The light moved slowly over the frozen field,
Over the dry seed-crowns,
The beautiful surviving bones
Swinging in the wind.[25]

A river glides out of the grass. A river or a serpent.
A fish floats belly upward,
Sliding through the white current,
Slowly turning,
Slowly.[26]

If the participles are given their full range, they turn such seemingly solid nouns as "bones" and "fish" into atemporal processes. Williams wanted a speaker beyond temporal constraints for the opening of Book II, and his satisfaction with the freedoms of the triadic stanza mostly consists in his having found a style answerable to the losses built into life itself. When he focuses on the full implications of the descent, readers are still aware of the differences in line-length, the enjambments, and the spacing that don't march in vertically straight columns. For Williams, the word "variable" in the phrase "variable foot" suggests limitless possibilities for the irregular, hanging, switchback line. And the speaker who lives in "The Descent" shapes himself with the line. He is capable of pausing and idling, and he is equally capable of moving forward in the space that surrounds him. Inside the moment of speech, an act comparable to a physical step, he is also outside of it, an activity inscribed by the potential of "walking." His mode of exploration is as endless as the descent it confronts.

Williams can be even more intricate and surprising. Throughout *Paterson*, but especially in Books II and III, his protagonist's search has been for crystallizations of language, "radiant gists" that contain and release the fullness of a city.[27] These moments are rare, but the purity of the search through the impurities of Paterson's topography and history remains firm. The phrase "radiant gist" comes from Williams's encounter with the work of Mme. Curie, a reference to her extracting, after years of work, a decigram of radium from tons of pitchblende. Paul Mariani traces Williams's fascination with the story to his viewing the film *Madame Curie* in 1944 and suggests that he transformed the search for radium into a guiding metaphor for his own discoveries in Book III.[28] Certainly the language of Book III, with its emphasis on the rigorous pursuit of beauty and unexpected manifestations of the "beautiful thing," offers a clue to his preoccupations. As Williams began to separate the luminous elements from the waste in preparation for Book III during the first months of 1948, Roethke published *The Lost Son and Other Poems* on March 11.[29] More than any book he would publish, *The Lost Son* defined Roethke's career. Williams had seen many of the poems in draft and most in their final form: he was well beyond the pleasure of first recognition. With *The Lost Son* in hand, he wrote to Roethke on April 10, 1948. Judged by standards of diplomacy, the letter surely fails. As a letter that attempts to isolate the core of Roethke's work, however, it reminds us of Williams's dedication to precision of feeling no matter what the cost:

Dear Ted:

I've had your book lying around, first on one table then on another. I've picked it up at odd moments, as one does trying to catch one's self off guard in order to get a sharp impression of a work. I've tried them early in the morning and late at night as well as in between. The pleasure I get is a formal one and, as far as I can see, that is the charm of the work.

There is the grotesque imagery and the mouldy coloring but the best of the work is I think in its formal tone, strictly in the line of the classic tradition. It's strange too for you, personally, don't signify that to me. Do you know Ford Madox Ford's poems? You remind me of him.

Such a thing, in spite of your prediction, as The Return pleases me more than the longer pieces which tend to break into isolated sequences. Somehow I think of Housman—even tho' it sets your teeth on edge to have me say so.

And that's about where I get off. Where the classic is paramount the thought governs the meter. It's your thought I like better than your verses, your verses as music that is. I think the music is conventional but in the thought there is a curious "decay" that is a just comment on your world. Baudelaire with his absolute honesty and unflinching stare at corruption and disease as inconsequential and part of the flesh (my own interpretation) had the same quality.

You are the sort of poet, to my taste, like Baudelaire, who by pol-
ishing the classic form to its last lustre will achieve his finest effects.

Maybe when we meet next, perhaps this summer tho' you may be
far from there in July, we can get a little soused and go further with
this first impression. A high polish seems at the moment something
you can do—as Brancusi did it with his bronze castings of the most
abstruse subjects.

I'm coming along as far as my illness goes, not yet able to drive a
car but walking about more or less as I please which isn't much. My
Papa's Waltz is effective. If that quality could be raised out of childhood into adulthood even more than you have raised it, savagely but
with impeccable perfection of surface, full rhyme and strictly measured lines it would win.

Sincerely,

Bill[30]

Compared with the advice he offered Roethke four years before
("Make it drunker, hotter, drippier. . . ."), Williams in this letter
seems to be taking a reactionary stance, as if he had put on
the mantle of a schoolmaster. "Formal tone" and "high polish"
are not values Williams had recommended for the success of
Roethke's art. Yet Williams, who often seems to develop in his
letters like a character in one of his novels, more exactly realizes
his meaning in the last paragraph when he speaks of Roethke's
potential for writing "savagely with impeccable perfection of surface," and he suggests that the fracture in Roethke's work can
only be healed by forcing the tendencies toward freedom and
discipline to their limits. This is advice of a peculiar kind. If offered by an analyst to an already distraught patient, it might
easily drive him into the wards. The compliment underlying this
advice, however, comes from Williams's belief that Roethke can
somehow hold these oppositions in balance. Beyond Baudelaire,
beyond Housman and Ford Madox Ford, Roethke's best poem lies
in wait, if he has the courage to move in its direction.

Such a crossgrained letter would become a test of friendship,
especially against the approval that began to gather for *The Lost*

Son. None of Roethke's major reviewers followed Williams. In *The New Yorker,* Louise Bogan praised the "ancient" pattern of "The Lost Son," finding the emotional curve of "light-found-after-darkness" especially satisfying.[31] Peter Viereck in the *Atlantic Monthly* commended Roethke's "original imagery" and singled out "the marvelously powerful rhythmic effect" of "The Shape of the Fire."[32] For Frederick Morgan in the newly established *Hudson Review,* the long poems of *The Lost Son* "represent an enormous advance over the earlier work. . . . Mr. Roethke has dramatized his materials by means of a dialogue between the "I" of the poems and answering voices, voices that may be variously identified but that possess in common with the witches in *Macbeth* and the washerwoman in the Anna Liva Plurabelle sequence of *Finnegans Wake* all the tough natural integrity of the animals and vegetation which they celebrate."[33] Roethke, who regarded praise of this kind as essential nourishment, did not respond with ease to Williams's remedy. It was as if Williams was trying to quarantine him within the walls of *Open House.* The situation was made more dramatic by Williams's expected arrival at the University of Washington two months hence. Roethke had invited him to read, to lecture, and to teach during the week-long Seattle Conference (July 19–25). By Williams's account, the conference was a "smacking success."[34] He lectured on "The Poem as a Field of Action," taught evening seminars, and read Paterson II to an audience of 150 enthusiastic listeners. Granville Hicks, another invited speaker, told him publicly that his audience would never forget him.[35] He also had two conversations with Roethke, the second on the last night of the conference, after the formalities were over. We know what was said, and more importantly what was not said, from a long letter that Williams wrote to Leota Willis, a colleague of Roethke's at the University of Washington. Ms. Willis had written to Williams immediately after the conference, probably at Roethke's behest, to ask Williams's opinion of the *long* poems. In recalling the conversation with Roethke, Williams remembers that he encouraged the poet who could design a poem by paradox, epigram, and an immediately perceived order:

August 3, 1948
(My grandson's sixth birthday)

Dear Mrs. Willis:

Replying to your inquiry about Ted's poems and referring particularly to the longer ones, I have sat here reading them over and over, from p. 45 (the last four poems in the book) for the past hour. I'm afraid I offended Ted when I saw him last week by saying that I liked the shorter ones better. I didn't feel like committing myself too far on what amounts to the development of the earlier, short poems. I can understand, naturally, how he resented this.

Every impetuous man wants to squeeze everything he desires to hear out of another's mind. He himself is full of himself—generously, of course—and is impatient when someone else whom he perhaps loves does not immediately respond in every minute detail to his desires. He feels that he has been rejected; that he has offered everything that is finest and has been thrown off. I told Ted what I could tell him, I wasn't ready to tell him anything else and I didn't tell him anything else—tho' I had earlier (on the first flash acquaintance with them) told him how much I admired certain lines of the longer poems.[36]

Not mentioned here is an incident Williams prominently mentioned in a private letter about the conference to Floss. At the end of this same conversation, Roethke had parted with Williams, taking with him a pint of Williams's Hennessey Three-Star brandy.[37] Whether Roethke took the brandy out of a lapse of memory or courtesy is not clear, but it is clear that his imagination did not fail him. The brandy, somehow, was meant to compensate for the blockages in the conversation and Williams's flat-minded views. Perhaps the bottle of Three-Star could remind him of the Williams he preferred to know—bracing and mellow. But Williams passes all that by. To Ms. Willis he writes that he has spent almost an hour reading the long poems and can see the filaments of the "modern" in them:

On reading the poems over and over, I have gradually been able to see how they have grown out of the shorter poems and how they have resolved those—until they have drained everything in them out of them and made them into whatever could be made of them—as much as can be made of anything by a poem. It is major work. The poems are a tremendous advance on the smaller poems. They are as fine, as masterly as any modern work I know. Absolutely serious in that seriousness which means to me all that a man can take seriously. They show also the great difficulty of creating a poem in the full modern sense.

Let me go further. I'd say there are very few serious poems in the full modern sense and that I am sure there is no poem worth paying attention to except the most modern, most aware in our day. Or the most modern in any day. I want to give the feeling of a very few imaginative works gradually approaching a difficult area which is to me the modern. To reach any such area the work must be athletic, tough and (whatever the man who writes a work chooses to be) without weakness. You've got to be in condition: the thing must be *made*, made to hold a life of its own with complete integrity into the rarified air it is forced to breathe to reach whatever summit. You don't get to the top with flabby muscles.

These last four poems have reached that area. They are spare and muscular—I don't see why we should ask more. But they are difficult. Well, why not? We've got to take them for what they are.

I know that what I've been saying so far is more or less metaphysical nonsense. I better get down to business. But damn it I'm not going to write a book, or a treatise on modern poems—it's easier to talk using figures.

But these are good poems and I've got to get down to business or confess that I'm lying. The gist is, if you wish, a common nostalgia for childhood—What answer can there be to that, that is for a man, but construction, invention in the finest mode. In other words the integrity of a man's technical overall making, building, constructing the poem itself is his answer. The poem itself is his answer.

So that if he builds well, newly he gives whatever ever answer a man and a poet can give. And if he "gives" it, by the excellence of his work, it is a gift. It is a gift to his day, to his people to whomever you choose to name. It is in short what is carelessly spoken of as love. If a man can't give his "love" he is a stick, a stone—Rather he is a defeated man. That is why we strive to create, to know, to write a poem. To have love, to give love we must work at the very limits of knowledge and of sweat and wit.

I say it's a difficult area to achieve. All kinds of devils pursue us. The same old difficulties that always beat us back when we try to beat the average figures in anything. All Ted's neuroses, his fears, his dreads and infantilisms—are nothing but a reflection of these difficulties. But if he writes a poem, in the full sense—then he lives and breathes again. I know his disappointments.

Alright. His language is clean. It is vivid. It closes up the sense often in two words. It is good music, refreshing and resourceful. Some of his images are brilliant—and moving. Look for instance at his freedom of musical sequence as compared with that of Robert Lowell.

Thus by the achievement of the poem a man changes a negative into a positive and becomes a rescuer of his times. Ted has done this but, as I say, there have been difficulties, the chief of which is that his—the bulk of his work is small, tenuous—and he seems to have exhausted his theme. He hasn't really. This is of nothing but temporary importance—tho' the difficulty is there.

He has achieved the poem—by what are to me the most able means—a musical, flexible line that breaks away from triteness, a pure objectivity of statement without pastiche of "explanation" or straining after effect. Just the opposite. His words are attached fast to the object and the object is "seen", always.

You feel all that is needed of the conventional line but it has been transformed from mere ritual into feeling, from all that is banal in conventional acceptance into sensation, into an emotional reality (a word that has to be raised with caution). As you know, knowing me, this in my opinion is the greatest virtue of all. Ted uses his own language, a felt language, not English but something much closer to us.

Perhaps his Prussian ancestry helps him in this, his German background. I think so and I think it one of the most important influences in our world. Not merely a German background because it is German, but a different background than English. It might be Spanish or

French—but here, in our use, it has shaken us free from triteness and the necessity for ritual and has permitted us to advance to the pure sensation, to the creation of the line in a truly basic sense. There are still very few intelligences who appreciate the importance of this— maybe not more than one or two. Ted has it, I don't say that he has fully as yet grasped how valuable it is.* (see below)

Individual lines in his poems are unbeatable but I have already spoken to him of this—graphic, succinct and wildly, beautifully imaginative. No one, at any time, has done better. This a poet must have— past all argument, figures, words, brilliance. He has all that.

He has a proper disrespect for the rhyme, something that in my opinion resembles more than anything else painted toe-nails. But graces have their uses, if we know what they are for. Emily Dickinson always makes you feel that the rhyme is secondary to something else. It is and may be profitably omitted in most cases or used as Ted uses them.

The individual 4 poems I'd value about as follows:

*(Note: *It has taken me a lifetime to discover this, to trace it to its sources, elucidate its implications and state them clearly. Ted did not come to my "lectures".)

A Field of Light—is, obviously, the lyric—the basic background. It is undisturbed and delightful tho' not the best.

The Lost Son—is, plainly, descriptive of the entering wedge, almost too literal. But after all the theme isn't to be hidden, why should it be? I'd say that Ted's dissatisfaction with this piece made him write the other two. I suppose he felt uncomfortable about having revealed too much. Or in not "getting over" the poem. Getting over the story but not the poem. He must have felt embarrassed about that.

That's always where the big step lies. To get out of oneself and make an object. Turn the thing inside out, get into the open and away from the mere subject. What such a poet as Auden does, or tries to do, when he writes an ecologue—or whatever he would do. Ted found himself too close to his own past—"His look drained the stones" is good but not as good as "Make the sea flash in the dust" from *The Long Alley*—which is a better poem, probably the best—tho' I am not sure.

It's all the same theme, that's the fault and the virtue of the book as a whole. There's a remembrance—dangerously narrow—and a struggle to escape and to *make*. To escape by making—which largely succeeds.

The last poem, *The Shape of the Fire*—with its very literal and successful lyric "Pleasure on ground" (tho' I dislike omitting the definite article in the place) is, again, and finally an attempt to define the "shape" and so get away from it. Rid one's self of it. "What's this? A dish for fat lips," is the Venus theme. He's afraid of it. Doesn't want it to cloud his vision of "quartz".

He wants to free himself from it. Again, he's got to be the poet. To make. Make new. If he can't he is lost.

And there we all are. His book has sold, showing it is more or less appreciated, that he has succeeded in something. He'd better be sure what it is—and not get fooled. And he does, at times, know.

That's all I have time for.

If you want to show this to Ted some time (that may even have been your intention in writing to me—or part of your intention I wish you would do so because I'm not going to say it again, to him or to anyone. I'd be glad to have you make a transcription of it if you would dare to take that much trouble and let him possess it. Because I think it is important to have men, women, tell each other—poets, that is—what they can of what they see. Most write "for the papers", a lot of crap—at the best.

Best luck[38]

W. C. Williams

The Williams who now commits himself to all of *The Lost Son* is also the Williams who lectured on "The Poem as a Field of Action" in Seattle, a lecture, he tells Ms. Willis, Roethke did not attend.

In every part, this reading of Roethke's poems takes place against
the background of the lecture. Throughout, Williams distinguishes between a rigidified tradition of formal utterance in poetry and the living language out of which the modern poem must
rise. Paul Mariani suggests that the lecture does not significantly
advance Williams's thought from the lecture at Penn State in 1940,
but the theory is more broadly applied, the examples are more
various, and the convictions more settled.[39] The examples are
mostly negative, poets who were right for their day but limited
as models for an age that has experienced the industrial revolution and the knowledge of relativity. Keats, Shelley and Tennyson
all express in their subject matter a wish for "aristocratic attain-
ment—a 'spiritual' bureaucracy of the 'soul' or what you will."[40]
Auden, a more complicated case, shows that his instincts were
right in coming to America, but his loyalty to conventional modes
traveled with him: he has been imprisoned by his skill in remembering them. Eliot, more complicated still, seeks to experiment,
yet finally his achievement rests with extraction and selection: "a
few poems beautifully phrased—in his longest effort thirty-five
quotations in seven languages."[41] For Williams the expression
"beautifully phrased" suggests no more than fastidious refine-
ment; when Eliot's finger points to the mountain, it always has a
sapphire ring on it. Against all this, Williams proposes a collective
"we," poets like Whitman who are so immersed in the vitality of
language that the language absorbs them. When Williams tries to
explain what he and the others actually do, his meanings release
themselves in participles:

> We are making a modern bolus: That is our somewhat undistin-
> guished burden; profusion, as, we must add in all fairness, against
> his (Eliot's) distinction.

> We are in a different phase—a new language—we are making the
> mass in which some other later Eliot will dig. We must see our oppor-
> tunity and increase the hoard others will find to use. We must find
> our pride in that. We must have the pride, the humility and the thrill
> in the making.

> We're not putting the rose, the single rose, in the little glass vase in

the window—we're digging a hole for the tree—and as we dig have disappeared in it.[42]

As in *Paterson II*, the participles challenge the distinction between subject and object until in the third passage, they achieve their end—the disappearance of "ourselves" in the transforming activity of work. The tree, which is directly related to the outcome of that work, holds Williams's vision of the poetry of the future: loyal to its place, relentless in its track of light, unself-conscious, perpetually "in the making."

His quest for a modernist poetic apart from Eliot's is always a part of his own quest for self-definition, but here it is made with the kind of confidence that borders on religious fervor. "In the making" offers a place to Roethke's activity in the long poem, just as it will offer an impetus to the energy of poets as different as Ginsberg and Lowell. Williams's emphasis on the imagination's open spaces and on their exploration should have made him an important reader of *The Lost Son*. In his letter to Ms. Willis, he has claimed that role, and his discussions of Roethke's work bring with them the implications of the lecture. Even his way of presenting himself as a reader bears a close relationship to the poem "in the making." The language of self-evolution ("I have gradually been able to see . . .") characterizes his understanding of himself and in part provides an answer for failing to grasp what he can now reach. Roethke's book is a kind of poem "in the making," the long poems amplifying the central experiences of the early work. Comparisons to the body's growth would be a natural guide for understanding such an achievement, so it is not surprising to meet this particular language in Williams's analysis. What is arresting is Williams's overturning much of his correspondence with Roethke by confronting the poems as objects that are special and at least momentarily finished. Metaphors of the body still shoulder Williams's meanings, but now the body is a young athlete's, with gravity, footing, tactility. For Williams, the best poems are "tough," and Roethke's last four poems are "spare" and "muscular." As he well knew, words such as "tough" and "muscular" have a history in American culture. William James would have recognized much of his own distinction between the "tender" and the "tough-minded" in Williams's language. His description of the "tough-minded" approach to experience—sensationalistic, materialistic, pluralistic, irreligious, fatalistic—shines a light on the temperament shared by Williams and Roethke.[43] Though both of them yearned on occasion for a universe explainable by a single principle, they returned again and again to the truth of "things" and the language of process and growth. Both believed that valuable work had been accomplished in recording the persistent ebullience of the world.

Noticeably absent in the letter is a phrase that has appeared in previous letters: "You remind me of. . . ." All those echoing voices Williams has heard in Roethke's other work (James Stephens . . . Baudelaire . . . Housman . . . Ford Madox Ford) fall silent before his admiration for *The Lost Son*. Other than the comment on Emily Dickinson's subtle use of rhyme, the only comparison Williams offers in the letter is Roethke's achievement in the music of the line paralleled with Robert Lowell's. For Williams, Lowell appears as an apprentice in the kind of work where Roethke has become a master. Quite a compliment when one considers that Williams's recent experiments in the music of the line make him into a critic of some standing. He is also willing to interrogate an earlier version of himself. When Williams observes that Roethke has achieved a "felt language" in part because his ancestry is "Prussian," he is refining one of his own favorite theories about the power of language that circulates in marketplace and street. He is almost certainly remembering Pound's comment on his own work written thirty years before:

> (You thank your bloomin gawd you've got enough Spanish blood to muddy up your mind, and prevent the current American ideation from going through it like a blighted collander.)
> The thing that saves your work is opacity, and don't you forget *it*. Opacity is NOT an American quality.[44]

Though Williams never speaks of Roethke's "opacity," he has in mind a similar characteristic: the state of being in shadow or darkness. Like Pound before him, Williams sees this as a laudable tendency. Clearly, he feels that there is some virtue in resisting the comfortable idioms of ordinary conversation. More, some special quality attaches to a poet like Roethke who encounters, and often enacts, what he cannot explain. What gives buoyancy to a poem, Williams implies, is what the poem leaves open, in the language and in the line. And that is where his accent finally falls. It is the line, which Williams never compares to anything inanimate, that fixes his attention. Moving in concert with the pitch and stress of conversation, the line, he believes, must also carry undertones of song; it must be supple and unforced; it must involve, as well, "something closer to us," a language bringing back, as he has already said in *Paterson I*, the "Earth, the chatterer, the father of all/speech." When Williams says in the letter that "it has taken me a lifetime to discover this," he refers to the line as the conductor of all these possibilities; the line is finally the small visible of a field of action. "Ted has it." Different as he and Roethke are, Williams suggests that both of them have a career ahead of them in forming, and reforming, the character of American poetry.

For most of the letter, Williams concentrates on the achievements of *The Lost Son*, but at the end he also reads its potentiality and assumes the mentor's role. There is still the poem Roethke hasn't written. Especially with "The Shape of the Fire," Williams finds traces of "the Venus theme" not faced, not brought into a persuasive relationship with a self he can recognize as complete. Finally, the poem Williams wants from Roethke is one that encompasses love and work, or more exactly, one that binds love, adult memory, and the sense of nature's presence into an exploration rather than an "escape." His reading of "The Shape of the Fire" suggests that the poem burns with two fires—sexual desire on the one hand and an impulse to connect the zest of the earth with the energies of the sun on the other—and that Roethke has not convincingly reconciled the two. Williams's response to all this is to "make new."

To a reader as sensitive as Roethke, the nuances of that phrase were not lost. Within a year, he had written one poem, "The Visitant," and begun a series of notebook entries that suggest he kept its meaning as a guide to the future.[45] "The Visitant" is about a young woman who has entered the speaker's life for a brief period and is now gone. In fact, she is the fantasy of a man who has fallen, or is falling, asleep, and she arrives mostly by way of negatives: "Her skirts not touching a leaf, / Her white arms reaching towards me / She came without sound, / Without brushing the wet stones."[46] When he awakens, however, he treats her as if she were just temporarily absent, someone who *might* re-appear. "Where's she now, I kept saying / Where's she now, the mountain's downy girl?"[47] The only answer that he receives comes from the willow tree that "swayed." At the end of the poem, he is alone with the willow's motion, paradoxically the veil of his desire and the solace of nature.

The notebook entries are starker and less contained by feelings of weight, limit, and wakefulness. They also record Roethke's openness to the powers of analogy, so strong at times that the speaker appears to be nothing more than a channel through which the language passes. In the following excerpts from Roethke's notebooks (1949–50), this relation is especially evident:

> She moved, gentle as a waking bird,
> Deep from her sleep, dropping the light crumbs,
> Almost silurian, into the lap of love . . .
> She moved, so she moved, gentle as a waking bird,
> The bird in the bush of her bones singing;
> Woke, from a deep sleep, the moon on her toes.
>
> Words for the wind, I know:
> She, dreamily lascivious, like a seed,
> Just new to sun and water, swelled within
> Until her deepest being had to heed
> The strict compulsion troubling all her skin.
>
> To find that, like a fish,
> What the fat leaves have—
> How else, meadow-shape?
> This fair parcel of summer's
> Asleep in her skin,
> A lark-sweet lover if ever there was.
> To the north of a mouth I lie
> Hearing a crass babble of birds:
> The water is busy
> In the place of beautiful stones;
> The fountain
> Hangs by its hair.[48]

Roethke is clearly turning outward here, focusing on the other as an incitement to "make new," but his success comes in moving the comparisons so far past their ordinary limit that they cannot be defined as a bridge to any further shore. In the first, nothing is stable, not even the speaker, who focuses twice ("She moved . . . so she moved") during the course of his elaborate comparison. "She" is moved by the comparison into a field of associations that touch history, sexual awakening, the unconscious, and the conflation of body and space. "The moon on her toes" becomes imaginatively convincing because the fusions in language have occurred all over the fragment: in the ambiguous pronoun references (whose "lap of love"?); in the merging of literal and figurative ("the bird in the bush of her bones singing"); in the participles that open the gate between past and present. The energy of all of these passages is the same energy that will turn Roethke into a distinguished maker of the love-lyric. Poems such as "Words for the Wind," "She," and "The Voice" complicate these fragments but they do not change the terms of engagement. In both, Roethke trusts the buoyancy of a resemblance to carry him to a new perspective of "she," the play of language changing him as well. It is as if the analogy moves with Dionysian excess and transport, releasing the subject from pictoral representation and the speaker from stasis and isolation. To "make new" brings with it another meaning as well. In the last of these excerpts, Roethke is less interested in the reach of a single analogy than the life of two generative images, acting like counterpointing themes in a fugue. The first is casually announced with the simile "like a fish." It is then dropped for the next five lines, surfacing again with "mouth," "babble," "water," and "fountain." The second is even more off-handedly introduced as part of a question: "How else, meadow shape?" In the next line, the "shape" becomes "this fair parcel" and will lead to "lark-sweet lover," "birds," "beautiful stones," and "hair." What these images share, what they illuminate in each other, is a kind of duplicitous innocence. Every one is erotically charged and part of a larger transformative process. By the time speaker and reader arrive at the "fountain" in the second last line, the word brings with it the sexual connotations of "mouth," the coloring of "beautiful

stones," the feminine implications of "water," and the spontaneity and audible flow inscribed in "crass babble." As an image
whose history begins in myth and legend, it also calls up the
worldwide belief that fountains are the source of youth and fertility, and the picture of fountains at the center of gardens, represen-
tative of a hallowed place. None of these interpretations is
privileged or final. Without losing its erotic ground, the passage
invites us to appreciate, in Roland Barthes's phrase, what plural
constitutes it.[49] Like the speaker, we are part of a field of action,
"in the making." With entries such as this, where readers find
themselves in widening circles of response, large as the imaginative encounter itself, Roethke begins his answer to Williams.

* * *

With Roethke's reading of Williams's letter, and his response to
it, the "mentoring" phase of their relationship comes to a close.
Williams's recognition of the achievement of the long poems is
his way of finding a place for them in the unfolding drama of
modernism. And Roethke will formalize his own recognition of
Burke's and Williams's enabling spirit by dedicating his next
book, *Praise to the End*, to "K. B. and W. C. W."[50] In recording
just their initials in the upper right-hand corner of his dedicatory
page, Roethke invites the reader to imagine the power of names
that remain mostly in shadow, and the blank page underneath
lengthens the mystery. Yet the page in Roethke's mind has been
amply filled. It expresses appreciation for the stimulating mix of
Burke's ideas, for the technique of "joycing," and for all those
unconventional perspectives Burke brought to their conversations. It contains a tribute to Burke's recommending "The Lost
Son" for publication in the *Sewanee Review*, a journal Williams
compared only half jokingly to the "big house."[51] It acknowledges
Burke's willingness in his seminal essay, "The Vegetal Radicalism
of Theodore Roethke," to find a history for Roethke's kind of
language in Dante's emphasis on the vernacular and infantile, in
Wordsworth's on the rustic, and in Lawrence's on the physical as
opposed to the "abstract."[52] To put it simply, Burke gave Roethke
a creditable past, a genealogy that would insure a hearing at

doors previously closed to him. He also gave Roethke wide recognition among serious readers of poetry. In the essay, Burke converts the movement of Roethke's long poems into the drama of regression and expectancy, the speaker's "struggle to avoid being undone" counterbalanced by moments when he seems to be on the verge of an "Ultimate Revelation."[53] Taken by themselves, these phrases might have stood as a critique of Eliot's longer poems, but Burke carefully distinguishes Roethke's drive for a language free of abstractions from Eliot's easy commerce with them, and he implies that this language will result in "a kind of phallic pantheism."[54] Such an effect is radically different from Eliot's swerve toward religious piety in the *Quartets*, and Burke underscores his engrossment in Roethke's work in the last half of his essay by looking back at the *Quartets* just twice; they become smaller and smaller, like a receding landmark. Burke's essay still occupies a central place in Roethke criticism, and Roethke himself immediately recognized the achievement. "I can only say that I never expected in my own life, that close and perceptive a reading," he wrote to Burke.[55] The reading also appeared in the Winter 1950 issue of the "big house," and it is not difficult to imagine what kind of emancipation it represented for Roethke.

Williams is a more elusive presence, but no less durable and continuing. In placing his initials next to Burke's, Roethke is recalling all of the roles—wise old man, doctor, explorer, comrade, schoolmaster, visionary, poet-as-maker—Williams assumed in the letters. He is also recalling Williams-as-reader, the Williams who told him his early work was blinkered, tame, and narcissistic, all the while suggesting that he learn from the eruptive language of Clytemnestra. Let it lead him back to the tensive relation between lost and found, where the self is discovered *en route*. Let it act on him as the wilderness acted on Boone: a primitive, unremitting challenge to go beyond whatever is reasonable or enclosed. And let it show him that enclosures can be subtle, like the greenhouse; or subtler, like the interference of self-consciousness; or subtler, like the urge to rest with an achieved style. Roethke is remembering Williams's genius for dissatisfaction, genius that, as Schopenhauer said, "hits a target . . . which others cannot even see."[56] The target is the poem Roethke himself could not immediately see, but it is also, over the course of his correspondence with Williams, a target that is moving: by turns, it is the next poem, the long poem, the poem "in the making," the poem that is "made." What Roethke could easily remember is that Williams did not want to solve the paradox of "making" and "made"; it brought the provocations which are the immediate life of poems. Lines are made and poems are occasionally finished, but another poem, perhaps it is *the* poem, fluid, open-ended, is always "in the making," becoming true. As it appears in Williams's letters, the phrase "make new" is finally a statement about power: the hidden but available vitality of a language that circulates through all of its speakers, but shows its strength in the mind of the poet; the capacity of a mind like Roethke's, or Williams's own, to convert what is ordinarily understood to be solid and "real" into a search for concealed energies, unsettled claims of attention; the demands of the poem, "a life of its own with complete integrity," where compelling transformations take place: the dreamer breaking all political bonds and desiring Russia or the walker losing himself in the walk. Roethke is remembering the Williams who could create a poem different from the formally designed, allusively layered poem and could thereby free the imagination for other poets to speak as well. It is the unaccommodated man, "my toughest mentor," who appears in those initials, the Williams waiting for the imagination's next move.

Notes

INTRODUCTION

1. William Carlos Williams, *I Wanted to Write a Poem* (New York: New Directions, 1978), 5.

2. Quoted in Ian Hamilton, *Robert Lowell* (New York: Random House, 1982), 234.

4. Theodore Roethke, *Selected Letters of Theodore Roethke,* ed. Ralph J. Mills, Jr. (Seattle: University of Washington Press, 1968), 101.

4. Williams to Roethke, Sept. 26,1941. Correspondence of William Carlos Williams and Theodore Roethke, Collection of American Literature, Beinecke Rare Book and Manuscript Library, Yale University. Hereafter designated YU. Previously unpublished material by William Carlos Williams copyright by William Eric Williams and Paul H. Williams; used by permission of New Directions Publishing Corporation, agents.

5. Most studies of Roethke give Williams no more than passing mention. See Richard Blessing, *Theodore Roethke's Dynamic Vision* (Bloomington: Indiana University Press, 1974); Don Bogen, *A Necessary Order: Theodore Roethke and the Writing Process* (Athens, Oh: Ohio University Press, 1991); Jennijoy LaBelle, *The Echoing Wood of Theodore Roethke* (Princeton: Princeton University Press, 1976); Karl Malkoff, *Theodore Roethke* (New York: Columbia University Press, 1966); Jay Parini, *Theodore Roethke: An American Romantic* (Amherst: University of Massachussetts Press, 1979); Lynn Ross-Bryant, *Theodore Roethke: Poetry of the Earth . . . Poetry of the Spirit . . .* (Port Washington, New York: Kennikat Press, 1981); Rosemary Sullivan, *Theodore Roethke: The Garden Master* (Seattle: University of Washington Press, 1975); Harry Williams, *The Edge is What I Have* (Lewisburg, Pa.: Bucknell University press, 1977); George Wolff, *Theodore Roethke* (Boston: G. K. Hall, 1981). In *William Carlos Williams: A New World Naked* (New York: McGraw-Hill, 1981), Paul Mariani quotes occasionally from Williams's side of the correspondence and he notices that Roethke's second book, *The Lost Son,* is a clear illustration of Williams's advice:"you've got to write more and more fully out of the less known side of your nature if you are to be noticed" (454). Within the context of two lives, however, the correspondence is so much more variegated than Mariani suggests that I have traced the sharp critical insights and the record of development that passed between them. James Breslin's *Something to Say: William Carlos Williams on Younger Poets* (New York: New Directions, 1985) contains an excellent, but brief, account of Williams's advice to Roethke between the publication of Roethke's first and second books. In his recent study of Roethke, *Theodore Roethke's Far Fields* (Baton Rouge: Louisianna State University Press, 1989), Peter Balakian has encountered several of the stylistic correspon-

dences between Williams and Roethke and has suggested that Roethke absorbed from Williams "a new sense of poetic language; a purified diction, a simpler syntax, a version of Williams's kinetic line measure, a concreteness of poetic perception and imagery, and a purer notion of 'organic metaphor'—stripped of allusion and intellectual reference" (37). What Balakian does not look into, however, is the spirited internal drama of the letters: the challenges, the criticisms, the silences, the rebuttals, the leaps, and the returns to seemingly missed connections. What Roethke learned was important, but the language by which it was passed,with accumulated meanings from Williams's previous letters, is equally important. The study I offer centers on Williams's involvement with Roethke's growth as an artist, with two variations. It is not always easy to know who learns from whom; or who, in the act of resisting the attitudes and opinions of the other, uncovers a rich layer of ambiguity in himself. In a word, the story is modern.

I am indebed to the bibliographic work on Roethke by James R. McLeod, *Theodore Roethke: A Manuscript Checklist* (Kent, Oh.: Kent State University Press, 1971); Ralph J. Mills, Jr., editor of the *Selected Letters of Theodore Roethke;* Keith R. Moul, *Theodore Roethke's Career: An Annotated Bibliography* (Boston: G. K. Hall and Co., 1977); and Randall Stiffler, *Theodore Roethke: The Poet and His Critics* (Chicago: American Library Association, 1986). Mariani's *William Carlos Williams* is an invaluable resource for information on Williams.

CHAPTER 1. "THE LESS KNOWN SIDE"

1. William Carlos Williams, *The Selected Letters of William Carlos Williams*, ed. John C. Thirlwall (New York: McDowell, Obolensky, 1957), 173–175.

2. William Carlos Williams, *Autobiography* (New York: New Directions, 1948), 310.

3. Allan Seager, *The Glass House* (New York: McGraw-Hill, 1968), 118.

4. The paper is dated May 12, 1940, and begins with a note in Roethke's writing: "Bill Williams to me after . . .", YU.

5. Williams to Roethke, Dec. 24, 1957, YU.

7. Theodore Roethke, *The Collected Poems of Theodore Roethke* (Garden City, N.Y.: Doubleday,1966), 27–28.

8. Jerome Mazzaro, *William Carlos Williams: The Later Poems* (Ithaca: Cornell University Press, 1973), 15–16.

9. Williams to Roethke, June 30, 1940, YU.

10. R. P. Blackmur, "Twelve Poets," *Southern Review* 7 (1941): 187.

11. Roethke to Williams, n.d., YU.

12. Williams to Roethke, Sept. 26,1941, YU.

13. William Carlos Williams, "Advice to a Young Poet," *View* 2, no. 4 (1942): 23.

14. Roethke, *Collected Poems*, 50.

15. Williams to Roethke, Sept. 22, 1942, YU.

16. William Carlos Williams, *Paterson* (New York: New Directions, 1963), 51.

17. LaBelle, *The Echoing Wood of Theodore Roethke*, 89.

18. Roethke, *Collected Poems*, 205.

19. *Harper's Bazaar*, November 1942, 25.

20. Roethke, *Selected Letters*, 101.

21. Ibid., 102, 106.

22. Ibid., 48.

23. Aeschylus, *The Oresteia*, trans. Robert Fagels (New York: Viking Press, 1966), 157.

CHAPTER 2. "THESE ARE THE BEST THINGS OF YOURS . . ."

1. Theodore Roethke, *Straw for the Fire*, ed. David Wagoner (Garden City, N.Y.: Doubleday, 1972), 147–159.

2. Roethke, *Letters*, 122.

3. Roethke, *Straw for the Fire*, 171, 178.

4. Roethke, *Collected Poems*, 37.

5. Roethke, *Letters*, 111.

6. Williams, *Autobiography*, Foreword, 3.

7. Mariani, *William Carlos Williams*, 492–493.

8. Williams to Roethke, July 2, 1944, YU.

9. Mariani, *William Carlos Williams*, 822n91.

10. Williams to Roethke, July 2, 1944, YU.

11. Williams to Roethke, July 14, 1944, YU.

12. Williams to Roethke , June 30, 1940, YU.

13. Roethke, "The Visitation" in Manuscripts Division, Box ROD-ROM, Theodore Roethke Folder, Department of Rare Books and Special Collections, Princeton University Library.

14. Roethke, *Collected Poems*, 108.

15. Roethke, *Letters*, 146.

16. Ralph Mills, in his note to this letter, quotes this sentence from Rodman's *100 American Poems*: "Roethke, like Kenneth Rexroth and Byron Vazakas, and to a lesser extent Elizabeth Bishop, derived his undressed and deceptively simple style from the cross-grained imagist, William Carlos Williams." Roethke, *Letters*, 146n3.

17. Seager, *The Glass House*, 148.

18. Roethke, *Straw for the Fire*, 147–169.

19. Roethke, *Collected Poems*, 56.

20. Roethke, *Letters*, 111.

21. Ibid., 111.

22. Allen Tate, "Seasons of the Soul," *Kenyon Review* 6 (1944): 1–9. Radcliffe Squires, in giving this poem a careful and sympathetic reading, concludes with this statement: " 'Seasons of the Soul' is not only a profound and distinguished poem. It is , at the level of formal art, one of the century's most magnificently sustained poems. And as one considers it in progress beginning with 'More Sonnets at Christmas,' he sees that Tate upped the ante with each poem, as if he supposed that the confusions of self and of the world could only be ordered by the most rigorous formality of art." Radcliffe Squires, *Allen Tate* (New York: Pegasus, 1971), 173–174.

23. Williams to Roethke, Nov. 14, 1944, YU.

24. Wallace Stevens, *Letters of Wallace Stevens,* ed. Holly Stevens (New York: Alfred A. Knopf, 1966), 246.

25. William Carlos Williams, *In the American Grain* (New York: New Directions, 1956), 9, 29, 113, 121, 137, 140, 157, 195, 200. See also William Carlos Williams, *Selected Essays* (New York: New Directions, 1969), 140–141.

CHAPTER 3. "THE LOST SON" AND "RUSSIA"

1. Roethke, *Selected Letters,* 122.

2. Kenneth Burke to Roethke, March 12, 1945, in the Theodore Roethke Collection, Suzzallo Library, University of Washington. Hereafter designated UW.

3. Yvor Winters, *Primitivism and Decadence* (London: Routledge and Kegan Paul, 1960), 46. Kenneth Burke, *A Grammar of Motives* (Berkeley: University of California Press, 1969), 48ln.

4. Roethke, Drafts of "The Lost Son," in Theodore Roethke Collection, Box 21, Folder 26, UW.

5. Seager, *The Glass House,* 41.

6. Frederick Schiller, *The Works of Frederick Schiller* (New York: Harvard Publishing Co., 1895), 1: 260.

7. Kenneth Burke, "What Are the Signs of What," *Language as Symbolic Action* (Berkeley: University of California Press, 1968), 361.

8. Roethke, *Collected Poems,* 54.

9. Ibid., 54.

10. Ibid., 57.

11. Ibid., 58.

12. Neal Bowers, *Theodore Roethke: The Journey from I to Otherwise* (Columbia: University of Missouri Press, 1982), 101–104.

13. Parini, *Theodore Roethke: An American Romantic,* 88.

14. Williams to Roethke, May 13, 1946, UW.

15. Ibid.

16. Williams, *Paterson,* 52.

17. William Carlos Williams, review of *The Granite Butterfly,* by Parker Tyler, *Accent* 6 no. 3 (1946): 203. The review is reprinted in James Breslin's *Something to Say,* 139–145.

18. T. S. Eliot, *The Complete Poems and Plays* (New York: Harcourt Brace and Co., 1952), 420.

19. Theodore Roethke, "Open Letter" in *Mid-Century American Poets,* ed. John Ciardi (New York: Twayne, 1950), 69.

20. Brendan Galvin, "Kenneth Burke and Theodore Roethke's 'Lost Son' Poems," *Northwest Review: Theodore Roethke Special Issue* 11, no. 3 (1971): 90–95.

21. Roethke, *Selected Letters,* 116.

22. Burke to Roethke, Nov. 24, 1945, UW.

23. Denis Donoghue, *Ferocious Alphabets* (New York: Columbia University Press, 1981), 206.

24. Burke to Roethke, Oct. 3, 1945, UW.

25. Williams to Roethke, May 13, 1946, UW.

26. Mariani, *William Carlos Williams*, 651–52.

27. William Carlos Williams, *The Collected Poems of William Carlos Willilams* (New York: New Directions, 1988), 2: 146–147.

CHAPTER 4. THE FIELD OF ACTION

1. Seager, *The Glass House*, 189.

2. Roethke, *Selected Letters*, 125.

3. Ibid., 124.

4. Williams, *Collected Poems*, 2:145.

5. Walt Whitman, *Leaves of Grass*, ed. Harold W. Blodgett and Scully Bradley (New York: New York University Press, 1965), 1.

6. Walter B. Kalaidjian, *Understanding Theodore Roethke* (Columbia: University of South Carolina Press, 1987), 70.

7. Balakian, *Theodore Roethke's Far Fields*, 88.

8. Sullivan, *Theodore Roethke: The Garden Master*, 101.

9.Parini, *Theodore Roethke: An American Romantic,* 101

10. Roethke, *Collected Poems*, 61.

11. Williams To Roethke, Dec. 3, 1946, UW.

12. Ransom's sentence is quoted in Kenneth Burke, "Key Words for Critics," *Kenyon Review* 4 (1942): 131.

13. Burke, "Key Words for Critics," *Kenyon Review*, 131.

14. John Crowe Ransom, "Poetry: The Formal Analysis," *Kenyon Review* 9 (1947): 436.

15. Although my characterization of the "walk" is somewhat different, I am indebted here to the parallel A.R. Ammons has drawn between poems and walks in "A Poem is a Walk," *Epoch* 18, no. 1 (1968): 117–119.

16. Williams, *Selected Letters*, 253,

17. Williams to Roethke, May 13, 1946, UW.

18. Williams, *Paterson*, 59.

19. Randall Jarrell, *Poetry and the Age,* (New York: The Ecco Press, 1953), 226.

20. Ibid., 261.

21. Carol Donley, "William Carlos Williams and 'Ol' Bunk's Band,' " *William Carlos Williams Review* 15, no. 2 (1989): 11.

22. Williams, *I Wanted to Write a Poem*, 80.

23. Williams, *Paterson*, 96–97.

24. Blessing, *Theodore Roethke's Dynamic Vision*, 73.

25. Roethke, *Collected Poems*, 58.

26. Ibid., 59

27. Williams, *Paterson*, 133.

28. Mariani, *William Carlos Williams*, 492.

29. Seager, *The Glass House*, 157.

30. Williams to Roethke, April 10, 1948, UW.

31. Louise Bogan, review of *The Lost Son*, *The New Yorker*, May 15, 1948, 118.

32. Peter Viereck, "Five Good Poets in a Bad Year, "*Atlantic Monthly* 182, no. 5 (1948): 95.

33. Frederick Morgan, "Recent Verse, "*Hudson Review* 1, no. 2 (1948): 262.

34. William Carlos Williams and James Laughlin, *Selected Letters*, ed. Hugh Witemeyer (New York: W.W. Norton, 1989), 156.

35. Mariani, *William Carlos Williams*, 564.

36. Williams to Leota Willis, Aug. 3, 1948, UW.

37. Mariani, *William Carlos Williams*, 564.

38. Williams to Leota Willis, Aug. 3, 1948, UW.

39. Mariani, *William Carlos Williams*, 564.

40. William Carlos Williams, *Selected Essays of William Carlos Williams* (New York: New Directions, 1954), 282.

41. Williams, *Selected Essays*, 285.

42. Ibid., 285–286.

43. William James, *Pragmatism* (Cambridge: Harvard University Press, 1975), 13.

44. Ezra Pound, *Selected Letters: 1907–1941*, ed. D. D. Paige (New York: New Directions, 1950), 124.

45. "The Visitant" was finished by Feb. 8, 1949. Roethke, *Selected Letters*, 148n.

46. Roethke, *Collected Poems*, 100.

47. Ibid., 101.

48. Roethke, *Straw for the Fire*, 57–58. These entries are all taken from the section entitled "In the Bush of Her Bones (1949–50)."

49. Roland Barthes *S/Z*, trans. Richard Miller (New York: Farrar, Straus and Giroux, 1974), 5.

50. Theodore Roethke, *Praise to the End* (Garden City, N.Y.: Doubleday, 1951), 5.

51. Burke to Roethke, Feb. 15, 1946, UW.

52. Kenneth Burke, "The Vegetal Radicalism of Theodore Roethke," *Sewanee Review* 58 (1950): 79.

53. Ibid., 86, 98.

54. Ibid., 105.

55. Roethke, *Selected Letters*, 160.

56. Arthur Schopenhauer, *The World as Will and Representation*, trans. E. F. J. Payne, 2 vols. (New York: Dover, 1966), 2: 391.

Bibliography

Aeschylus. *The Oresteia.* Translated by Robert Fagels. New York: Viking, 1966.

Ammons, A. R. "A Poem is a Walk." *Epoch* 18, no. 1 (1968): 114–119.

Balakian, Peter. *Theodore Roethke's Far Fields.* Baton Rouge: Louisiana State University Press, 1989.

Barthes, Roland. *S/Z.* Translated by Richard Miller. New York: Farrar, Straus and Giroux, 1974.

Blackmur, Richard P. "Twelve Poets." *Southern Review* 7 (1941): 187–213.

Blessing, Richard. *Theodore Roethke's Dynamic Vision.* Bloomington: Indiana University Press, 1974.

Bogan, Louise. Review of *The Lost Son,* by Theodore Roethke. *The New Yorker* May 15, 1948: 118.

Bogen, Don. *A Necessary Order: Theodore Roethke and the Writing Process.* Athens, Oh.: Ohio University Press, 1991.

Bowers, Neal. *Theodore Roethke: The Journey from I to Otherwise.* Columbia: University of Missouri Press, 1982.

Breslin, James. *Something to Say: William Carlos Williams on Younger Poets.* New York: New Directions, 1985.

Burke, Kenneth. *A Grammar of Motives.* Berkeley: University of California Press, 1969.

———. "Key Words for Critics." *Kenyon Review* 4 (1942): 126–132.

———. *Language as Symbolic Action.* Berkeley: University of California Press, 1968.

———. Letters to Theodore Roethke. March 12, 1945. February 15, 1946. Theodore Roethke Collection. Suzzallo Library, University of Washington.

———. "The Vegetal Radicalism of Theodore Roethke." *Sewanee Review* 8 (1950): 68–108.

Donley, Carol. "William Carlos Williams and '01' Bunk's Band.'" *William Carlos Williams Review* 15, no. 2 (1989): 9–16.

Donoghue, Denis. *Ferocious Alphabets.* New York: Columbia University Press, 1981.

Eliot, T. S. *The Complete Poems and Plays.* New York: Harcourt Brace and Co., 1952.

Galvin, Brendan. "Kenneth Burke and Theodore Roethke's 'Lost Son' Poems." *Northwest Review: Theodore Roethke Special Issue* 11, no. 3 (1971): 67–96.

Hamilton, Ian. *Robert Lowell.* New York: Random House, 1982.

James, William. *Pragmatism.* Cambridge: Harvard University Press, 1975.

Jarrell, Randall. *Poetry and the Age*. New York: The Ecco Press, 1953.

Kalaidjian, Walter. *Understanding Theodore Roethke*. Columbia: University of South Carolina Press, 1987.

La Belle, Jennijoy. *The Echoing Wood of Theodore Roethke*. Princeton: Princeton University Press, 1976.

Levertov, Denise. *The Poet in the World*. New York: New Directions, 1960.

Malkoff, Karl. *Theodore Roethke*. New York: Columbia University Press, 1966.

Mariani, Paul. *William Carlos Williams: A New World Naked*. New York: McGraw Hill, 1981.

Mazzaro, Jerome. *William Carlos Williams: The Later Poems*. Ithaca: Cornell University Press, 1973.

McLeod, James R. *Theodore Roethke: A Manuscript Checklist*. Kent, Oh.: Kent State University Press, 1971.

Morgan, Frederick. "Recent Verse." *Hudson Review* 1, no. 2 (1948): 258–266.

Moul, Keith R. *Theodore Roethke's Career: An Annotated Bibliography*. Boston: G. K. Hall and Co., 1977.

Parini, Jay. *Theodore Roethke: An American Romantic*. Amherst: University of Massachusetts Press, 1979.

Poirier, Richard. *Robert Frost: The Work of Knowing*. N.Y.: Oxford University Press, 1977.

Pound, Ezra. *Selected Letters: 1907–1941*. Edited by D. D. Paige. N.Y.: New Directions, 1950.

Ransom, John Crowe. "Poetry: The Formal Analysis." *Kenyon Review* 9 (1947): 436–456.

Roethke, Theodore. Biographical Note. *Harper's Bazaar* November 1942: 25.

———. *The Collected Poems of Theodore Roethke*. Garden City, N.Y.: Doubleday, 1966.

———. Letter to William Carlos Williams. No date. Begins with: "Here's that ballad I was blowing about. It was set up . . ." Correspondence of William Carlos Williams and Theodore Roethke. Beinecke Rare Book and Manuscript Library, Yale University.

———. Letter to William Carlos Williams. No date. Begins with: "Old Dick the Prick . . ." Correspondence of William Carlos Williams and Theodore Roethke. Beinecke Rare Book and Manuscript Library, Yale University.

———. "The Lost Son": Drafts. Theodore Roethke Collection. Suzzallo Library, University of Washington.

———. "Open Letter." *Mid-Century American Poets*. Edited by John Ciardi. N.Y.: Twayne, 1950. 67–72.

———. *Praise to the End*. Garden City, N.Y.: Doubleday, 1951.

———. *Selected Letters of Theodore Roethke*. Edited by Ralph J. Mills, Jr. Seattle: University of Washington Press, 1968.

———. *Straw for the Fire*. Edited by David Wagoner. Garden City, N.Y.: Doubleday, 1972.

———. "The Visitation." Manuscripts Division. Department of Rare Books and Special Collections. Princeton University Library, Princeton University.

Ross-Bryant, Lynn. *Theodore Roethke: Poetry of Earth . . . Poetry of Spirit.* Port Washington, N.Y.: Kennikat Press, 1981.

Schiller, Frederick. *The Works of Frederick Schiller.* Vol. 1. Harvard. Publishing Co., 1895.

Schopenhauer, Arthur. *The World as Will and Representation.* Translated by E. F. J. Payne. Vol. 2. N.Y.: Dover, 1966.

Seager, Allan. *The Glass House.* New York: McGraw Hill, 1968.

Squires, Radcliffe. *Allen Tate.* New York: Pegasus, 1971.

Stevens, Wallace. *Letters of Wallace Stevens.* Edited by Holly Stevens. New York: Alfred A Knopf, 1966.

Stiffler, Randall. *Theodore Roethke: The Poet and his Critics.* Chicago: American Library Association, 1986.

Sullivan, Rosemary. *Theodore Roethke: The Garden Master.* Seattle: University of Washington Press, 1975.

Tate, Allen. "Seasons of Soul." *Kenyon Review* 6 (1944): 1–9.

Viereck, Peter. "Five Good Poets in a Bad Year." *Atlantic Monthly* 182, no. 5 (1948): 95–97.

Whitman, Walt. *Leaves of Grass.* Edited by Harold W. Blodgett and Scully Bradley. New York: New York University Press, 1965.

Williams, Harry. *The Edge is What I Have.* Lewisburg, Pa.: Bucknell University Press, 1977.

Williams, Williams Carlos. "Advice to a Young Poet." *View* 2, no. 4 (1942): 23.

———. *Autobiography.* New York: New Directions, 1948.

———. *The Collected Poems of William Carlos Williams.* Edited by Christopher MacGowan. 2 vols. New York: New Directions, 1988.

———. *I Wanted to Write a Poem.* New York: New Directions, 1978.

———. *In the American Grain.* New York: New Directions, 1956.

———. Letter to Leota Willis. Aug. 3, 1948. Theodore Roethke Collection. Suzzallo Library, University of Washington.

———. Letters to Theodore Roethke. June 30, 1940. Sept. 26, 1941. Sept. 22, 1942. July 2, 1944. July 14, 1944. Nov. 14, 1944. Dec. 24, 1957. Correspondence of William Carlos Williams and Theodore Roethke. Beinecke Rare Book and Manuscript Library, Yale University.

———. Letters to Theodore Roethke. May 13, 1946. Dec. 3, 1946. April 10, 1948. Theodore Roethke Collection. Suzzallo Library, University of Washington.

———. Paper to Theodore Roethke. May 12, 1940. Correspondence of William Carlos Williams and Theodore Roethke. Beinecke Rare Book and Manuscript Library, Yale University.

———. *Paterson.* New York: New Directions, 1963.

———. Review of *The Granite Butterfly,* by Parker Tyler. *Accent* 6, no. 3 (1946): 203–206.

———. *Selected Essays of William Carlos Williams.* New York: New Directions, 1954.

———. *Selected Essays.* New York: New Directions, 1969.

————. *The Selected Letters of William Carlos Williams.* Edited by JohnC. Thirlwall. New York: McDowell, Obolensky, 1957.

————and James Laughlin. *Selected Letters.* Edited by Hugh Witemeyer. New York: W. W. Norton, 1989.

Winters, Yvor. *Primitivism and Decadence.* London: Routledge and Kegan Paul, 1960.

Wolff, George. *Theodore Roethke.* Boston: G. K. Hall, 1981.

Index